Praise for *The Most Important Point*

"These talks really capture the modesty and down-to-earth reality of Dōgen and Suzuki Roshi's, and now Ed Brown's, Zen. I was deeply touched by them. One recipe after another for true practice, if you are ready to cook and be cooked. Enjoy!"

JON KABAT-ZINN
founder of MBSR and author of *Falling Awake*

"This is a book that will nourish all aspects of one's life. Smart, sharp, deep, like a good meal, the wisdom that Ed Espe Brown offers us is a treasure for all time. And it makes Zen digestible, even delicious!"

ROSHI JOAN HALIFAX
abbot of Upaya Zen Center and author of *Standing at the Edge*

"Suzuki Roshi once said, 'The most important point is to find out what is the most important point.' After a lifetime of practice inspired by his teacher, Suzuki Roshi, Ed Brown has discovered that the most important point is love and acceptance. No one expresses this most important point better than Ed. His simple, soulful, honest talks will melt your heart."

NORMAN FISCHER
poet, Zen priest, and author of *Experience:
Thinking, Writing, Language, and Religion*

"Ed and Danny, two master chefs, have prepared a simple and elegant literary feast—with Tassajara magic for its background flavor. Humor and well-chosen poems add juice to dish after dish. *The Most Important Point* does not shy away from relating raw personal experiences with warmth and compassion. I have no doubt that many readers will find this book, as I have found it page after page, irresistible."

BROTHER DAVID STEINDL-RAST
Benedictine monk, author of *Gratefulness, the Heart of Prayer: An Approach to Life in Fullness* and *May Cause Happiness: A Gratitude Journal*, and cofounder of gratefulness.org

"Like the best teaching in any spiritual tradition, *The Most Important Point* speaks to you just where you are. If you're new to Zen, this book is for you. If you've been practicing a long time, this book is also for you. It is filled with the wisdom of a lifetime."

RUTH OZEKI
author of *A Tale for the Time Being* and *The Face*

"No matter what you think you know about Zen, Ed Brown may know more. He certainly prepares his wisdom like a meal: pungent, saturated with taste, leaving very little to discard. He makes it look easy. I couldn't put this book down. It made me feel like a beginner all over again . . . after 45 years."

HOSHO PETER COYOTE
author and Zen priest

"Brilliant, humorous, and heartwarming."

VANJA PALMERS
Zen teacher, founder of Felsentor Meditation Center

the Most Important Point

Also by Edward Espe Brown

The Tassajara Bread Book

Tassajara Cooking

The Tassajara Recipe Book

Tomato Blessings and Radish Teachings

The Complete Tassajara Cookbook

Not Always So

No Recipe

the
Most
Important
Point

Zen Teachings of
Edward Espe Brown

edited by
Danny S. Parker

sounds true
BOULDER, COLORADO

Sounds True
Boulder, CO 80306

Published 2019

Cover design by Lisa Kerans
Book design by Beth Skelley

Cover photograph by Thomas Radlwimmer

Part I opening photo by Ko Blix. Part IV opening photo by Frank Espe
Brown. All other photos courtesy of the author's private collection.

Printed in Canada

Library of Congress Cataloging-in-Publication Data

Names: Brown, Edward Espe, author. | Parker, Danny S., editor.
Title: The most important point : Zen teachings of Edward Espe Brown /
   edited by Danny Parker and Edward Espe Brown
Description: Boulder, CO : Sounds True, Inc., 2019.
Identifiers: LCCN 2018016734 (print) | LCCN 2018042133 (ebook) |
   ISBN 9781683642428 (ebook) | ISBN 9781683641605 (pbk.)
Subjects: LCSH: Zen Buddhism.
Classification: LCC BQ9266 (ebook) | LCC BQ9266 .B56 2019 (print) |
   DDC 294.3/927—dc23
LC record available at https://lccn.loc.gov/2018016734

10 9 8 7 6 5 4 3 2 1

For our beloved teachers:
Shunryu Suzuki,
Dainin Katagiri,
and Kobun Chino.
And to the spirit of Zen
they embodied.

The most important point
is to find out
what is the most important point.

SHUNRYU SUZUKI ROSHI

Contents

Preface

I met Edward Espe Brown in the summer of 1974 at San Francisco Zen Center. Our introduction was fleeting and unremarkable.

I was a twenty-one-year-old kid who had read about Zen practice and, for reasons I could not explain, was magnetically drawn to the teachings of Shunryu Suzuki Roshi. Ed was part of the "in-crowd" at Zen Center, where I was a youthful spiritual seeker, otherwise anonymous and chronically naïve. Indeed, I spent months in the charge of Philip Whalen without realizing he was a famous Beat poet!

My experience with Zen practice during those months was surprising and largely disappointing—not at all what I had imagined. Nothing in my life was solved. My problems loomed larger than when I first came. Far from reaching enlightenment, I experienced my life as patently mundane. The magic carpet of *kensho* (sudden awakening) was pulled out from under me. The great hope for a big transformative realization was gone.

Yet leaving Zen Center, I remained curiously drawn to zazen, the practice of meditation, and continued that for years—even teaching it. But, as it happens, I slowly drifted away from practice in the 1980s and became bitter and morose.

I skated the edges of alcoholism, cynicism, divorce. I didn't like myself at all.

It was during that time, 1993 to be exact, that grace came in the form of a close bond with a sudden new friend, John Busch, from Lawrence Berkeley National Laboratory. John mentioned that he was sitting Zen meditation with Ed Brown at Green Gulch Farm near Sausalito. I remembered Ed and Zen. Maybe I should try that again. On John's invitation, I attended one of Ed's one-day sittings.

It was a simple event but remains one of the most powerful and pivotal of my life. Practicing with Ed that day was at once revealing and cathartic. What was happening to me? My life seemed to explode in a powerful mix of emotion and expanded awareness. Old pinecones falling periodically on the metal roof thumped like a steady cheering section; outdoors, jays wailed for me. Even my aching legs seemed to love me. I was home again in quiet, simple kindness.

Ed was humble, human, real. No cardboard Zen master spouting sutras and koans, he was a deeply caring man who made me feel welcome in the world of deeply flawed human beings. He was flawed too—he made that clear. He seemed to speak directly to me. Maybe being messed up was okay. Tears streamed down my face.

Suddenly, I knew why I had left Zen practice. I was poorly skilled at it—or at least I thought I was. Still, the deep revelation of that day of simple sitting with a warm and genuine heart left me feeling that being vulnerable might be okay. I might be able to fall in love with life again. I knew—was completely certain—that, even if unskilled, I would never again leave Zen practice. I would do this practice until my final day.

A person who is dedicated yet poorly skilled likely needs a teacher. I followed Ed around to events and retreats. One summer afternoon at Tassajara Zen Mountain Center, I asked for a meeting—something I had been too intimidated to attempt with other Zen teachers. When we met, I blurted out my certainty, "I will never quit Zen practice again." Then I acknowledged, "But I am really bad at it. I need help."

I made my confession to Ed just outside the beautiful Kaisando, a place of tribute to the founder of this monastery, his teacher Suzuki Roshi. The late afternoon scene was filled with a gold western light. Ed's eyes were close to mine.

"Go wash your face, young man." He spoke quietly and encouraged me to come back later for tea. "I have chocolate," he added.

Ed was reluctant to accept another student: too many failures on both sides. But I was insistent, and he took me on.

Now, years later, I am deeply indebted to my teacher, who saw fit to ordain me as a priest in 2011. I want to share with you some of the many beautiful things I have learned from him. For me, Ed has breathed real life into Zen practice, which all too often suffers from its staid Japanese origins, where emotion is expunged and willingness to experiment can be squeezed out by adherence to fixed forms.

"How will you experience this life, moment after moment?" Ed once asked me. "Are you willing to have what is there?"

Before my mind could protest, he made a suggestion: "Will you sit in the middle of your life, right in the middle, and experience what is there?" He said it was like a fire, but if you practice with zazen itself, you might get the chance to sit still for what life has to offer. Right in the middle of the fire of your life.

This book manifests Ed Brown's teachings. And they are various. Because Ed was the illustrious and temperamental *tenzo* (head cook) at Tassajara Zen Mountain Center for two and a half years and has studied cooking and food his entire adult life, you will find a lot about Zen wisdom as well as food and what it means to "cook your life"—in his words.

The truth is you're already a cook.
Nobody teaches you anything,
but you can be touched, you can be awakened.
Put down the book and start asking,
"What have we here?" you come to your senses.
Though recipes abound, for soups and salads,
breads and entrées, for getting enlightened
and perfecting the moment, still
the unique flavor of Reality
appears in each breath, each bite,
each step, unbounded and undirected.
Each thing just as it is,
What do you make of it?[1]

It was the wish of Ed's teacher, Shunryu Suzuki Roshi, that in coming to North America, Zen Buddhist practice might well be transformed into vibrant new forms that would revitalize an ancient tradition. Ed exemplifies that transformative view.

"See what you can find out," Suzuki urged. "The most important point is to find out what is the most important point!"

Ed Brown urges the same, as you will see.

---

1 Edward Espe Brown, *The Complete Tassajara Cookbook: Recipes, Techniques, and Reflections from the Famed Zen Kitchen* (Boston: Shambhala, 2009), 242.

I am so pleased to bring Ed's teachings forward. I wish for you the bounty that will almost certainly emerge as you find the most important point in your own life. Even if this modest volume is but a small aid in that journey, that will be quite enough.

Warm wishes,
Danny Parker
Shōjō Reigen
August 2016

I

You Can't Always Get
What You Want

Wild West Tassajara

I first came to Tassajara the summer of 1966. My friend Alan Winter had gone on a Zen Center ski trip—I think it was the last Zen Center ski trip—in the spring of 1966 and met someone named Richard Baker. Richard told Alan that Zen Center was thinking about buying some land down here at Tassajara. Zen Center had about $1000 in the bank. He told my friend there was this place called Tassajara and "Why don't you get a job there?" So Alan got a job at Tassajara as a handyman. He told me I could probably get a job in the kitchen, which I did.

The kitchen was where the pit is now. It was a pretty nice kitchen, with an open-air tower at the top so a breeze could come through. Today's student eating area was the bar. For many years, Tassajara was a destination drinking spot. You'd drive the fourteen-mile dirt road, get a drink, and go to the hot tubs. Those were the days. The Tassajara dining room was where the kitchen is now. Bob and Anna Beck, the owners of Tassajara at the time, lived where the dining room is now; previously it had been divided into rooms.

As always it was hot in the summer. When you worked in the kitchen, you could order a Carta Blanca or a Dos Equis from the bar. Some cooks would have a gin and tonic with a twist of lime. If you were a cook, you wanted to stay cool and in good humor. Maybe it helped take the edge off.

Once our nearest neighbor drove the fourteen-mile dirt road all the way down into Tassajara. To get our attention, he drove his VW bug in a big circle in the parking lot, spinning his wheels and firing off his gun into the air.

I went out to check on the commotion. "Hey, Bill, can I get something for you?" I asked.

"I'm thirsty."

I offered him some Carta Blanca beer.

"Beer? Got any whiskey?"

After I'd brought out some glasses and a bottle labeled whiskey, he spit it out. "This isn't whiskey," he said, "it's Scotch."

That being corrected soon enough, after a drink or two, he was on his way.

I had a job washing dishes and scrubbing pots. Jimmie and Ray were making beautiful bread, so I asked, "Will you teach me?"

They said, "You bet."

Then I was dishwasher, pot scrubber, and baker. About halfway through the summer, one of the cooks quit. Bob and Anna then asked me, "Why don't you be the cook?" So I started cooking. That was the summer of 1966. I had two and a half months of experience cooking.

That fall, Zen Center arranged to buy Tassajara for $300,000. We had to raise $25,000 for a down payment. We had garage sales and car washes and a "Zenefit." The posters in San Francisco said "ZENEFIT" and showed the silhouette of one of the mountains from the ridge above Tassajara. Quicksilver Messenger Service, Jefferson Airplane, and Big Brother and the Holding Company played a benefit concert for the San Francisco Zen Center in the Avalon Ballroom. There were hundreds of people. I think the tickets were four or five dollars. During a break in the music, Suzuki Roshi gave a talk to the hundreds of stoned hippies. We raised $1,800 from that Zenefit.

That winter there were three or four caretakers at Tassajara from the Zen Center. I have not, to this day, heard what happened, but they thought we needed to have a new kitchen before the next guest season. This was not accurate information, but they believed that to be true. They were not in close communication with the Zen Center in the city, as the phone was on a single wire running through the woods—if there was a storm and a branch fell on it, service was down until someone walked the line. In whatever state they were in, from whatever they were consuming, the caretakers decided, "We need a new kitchen before we open next year, so we'd better tear down the old one."

When we got down there the following April, what was left of the kitchen was a platform. There were three walk-in refrigerators left at the far side of the platform. You opened them at night to let cold air in and closed them during the day to keep it there. Refrigeration in the summer was down to about seventy rather than ninety degrees during the day.

The new temporary kitchen was where the dish shack is now. It had been the crew's dining room. Two people could pass around the central table if they turned sideways. There was a counter at the end, two stoves that are in the kitchen now, a smaller stove, a gas refrigerator, one little sink, and a whole wall of shelves. We built a storeroom outside, which is gone now. We did dishes outside on the porch. Brother David Steindl-Rast, a Benedictine monk, was the first dishwasher for the first practice period in the summer of 1967.

I attended the first seven practice periods at Tassajara in the old zendo, the meditation hall, which had been the bar. The dining room was torn down, and we started working on a new kitchen. We did everything ourselves. The first septic tank we dug by hand. It took weeks. Now we know to bring in a backhoe.

So I was at the first seven practice periods, at eleven of the first thirteen practice periods, and at Tassajara for the first seven summers. Three of those summers I worked in the kitchen. One summer I worked in the office. One summer I did stonework, and I was *shika* (the guest manager) for another.

The teachers I practiced with are gone now. Three of the seven *shusos* (head students) who led the first seven practice periods are also gone. The zendo I sat in isn't there any longer. The kitchen I worked in isn't there. We are only here for a few more moments—maybe not even a few more. Maybe this is our last moment. Suzuki Roshi, one morning when we were sitting, said: "Don't move. Just die over and over. Don't anticipate. Nothing can save you now, because this is your last moment. Not even enlightenment will help you now, because you have no other moments. With no future, be true to yourself—and don't move."[2]

What is it to be true to your self? We think the way to go through life is to create a picture of how we should be. We don't consciously create it, but we have it. We know how to be according to what we've been through, what we have experienced. We know how we should be so that we will get approval and avoid criticism and punishment. What do we need to do?

2 Edward Espe Brown, verbal memory. Quoted in *Zen Is Right Here: Teaching Stories and Anecdotes of Shunryu Suzuki,* ed. David Chadwick (Boulder, CO: Shambhala, 2007), 33.

It never works, does it? Abandoning yourself to gain recognition. Has it been working lately? You go through life putting on your best performance, yet something doesn't work. People still may not be happy with you. They have a problem. You have a problem. You are not the way you are supposed to be. You think that if you were spiritual and enlightened, then you wouldn't have the problems you are having, would you?

What do you suppose it's good for—this spirituality, this enlightenment, this realization? You think, *I will get it. I will have it. I will do what I need to do to get it. How do I perform so I look good, look spiritual, and everybody begins to approve of and recognize me for the masterful spiritual being that I am?*

There are various problems with this. For one, it doesn't work. You're doing the best you can. You're trying to be happy, buoyant, cheerful, calm, peaceful. *Don't get angry. Watch out for desire. Don't have any preferences.* See if you can regulate your mind. *Ah, I did it. I got my mind just the way it is supposed to be, and I have kept it that way for eighteen years.* You've got a grip on yourself, rather than a spiritual life.

Of course, you cannot do this. You cannot keep the mind you think you are supposed to have while you keep having experiences that you told yourself you weren't going to have anymore. It's like failed New Year's resolutions.

The other problem with this: If you got all that approval, what would it be good for? Who cares? How will you get out of this worrying about audience approval?

It's like Calvin of *Calvin and Hobbes* going to his dad and saying, "Dad, your approval ratings are down."

His dad says, "Excuse me, Calvin, but I'm not aiming for high approval ratings. I'm aiming to raise you to be a good person."

And Calvin says, "Your approval ratings are not going to improve with that attitude."

The other problem here is that you are missing what you truly long for. What do you long for most deeply? What do human beings long for? It's your heart. Something comes into your heart and touches you. Your heart extends out to meet others and the world. Then the world and others and you come into your heart.

You think, *I could love myself if I got enough approval.* And when will that be? Maybe you could just go ahead and love somebody who doesn't quite measure up—the person you are, who doesn't quite measure up. Maybe you could go ahead and have a kind feeling, a tenderhearted feeling for this poor, miserable person, who still doesn't measure up, still hasn't gotten anywhere, still isn't always calm, patient, tolerant, blissful, buoyant, cheerful, kind.

Over and over again, I have shifted. How do I have a tender feeling for myself? At some point, what is in your heart? What is your deep wish, the most important point, as Suzuki Roshi called it? What is the most important point? You answer, not once and for all, but simply for right now. What is it? You might have a feeling, a thought, a sensation. You might get a little hint. When you keep listening, your heart reveals itself more and more. *What is most important?* Something comes to you when you ask.

Suzuki Roshi was not masterful, except when he chose to be. Occasionally, he thought telling us something might help us—"Don't move. Just die." I was talking with Alan Winter on the bridge. He was remembering when there were no benches and only a little wooden railing. Back in the sixties or early seventies, Suzuki Roshi was standing on the bridge when Alan came through with a group of friends from the Narrows, a deep rocky canyon made by the winding path of Tassajara Creek two miles east of the monastery.

Suzuki Roshi turned around and looked at them and smiled, and Alan said he felt deeply received, met, and seen. Many of us had this experience with Suzuki Roshi.

Beyond your performance, who are you? Maybe you can find a tender, vulnerable, good-hearted person—also boundless and vast—who is ready to see and be seen, someone who is ready to smile.

Easy Is Right

Funny thing—you start sitting, and your life unfolds. Sitting meditation is beyond your conception, beyond your agency. It's beyond your doing or structuring. You sit down here, and your life unfolds without your directing it. That's the good news, and the bad news: it's out of your control. And isn't that great? If it were up to you to control things, how utterly challenging that would be with so many things "misbehaving." You might not appreciate their liveliness while you are busy wanting them to be peaceful, calm, or serene. Your life opens up and you become more interested in how things are manifesting, as you stop telling them to be different than they are.

To talk about posture, I'd like to mention a Taoist saying by Chuang Tzu. He said: "Easy is right. Begin right, and you are easy. Continue easy, and you are right. The right way to go easy is to forget the right way, and to forget the way is easy." Ease is one of the traditional Buddhist virtues. Ease is a feeling of happiness or well-being, a sense of making yourself at home in your body and mind and welcoming your experience home to your heart.

There are different points of view about home. How do you make yourself at home in your body? One way is to make it a comfortable place to hang out. You help your body find its stability so that you can feel at home and be easy in it. "Begin right, and you are easy." You begin by establishing your stability and balance, and then you have ease. "Continue easy, and you are right." This is different from *How do I do this right?* (as though right were something moral or conceptual that you could judge right or wrong, good or bad). You could be at ease, and Chuang Tzu says that to be at ease is right. Make yourself at home in your body and then welcome your experience home to your heart, into your being.

This welcoming attitude is a bit of a stretch for some of us because the things that come along are not all welcome. Some of them you'd just as soon they would go away. But this is a different sense of welcoming. It's like the Rumi poem that says, "Every morning a new arrival / A joy, a depression, a meanness . . . / Welcome and entertain them all! Even if they are here to clean you out."[3]

Begin right, and you will have ease. Continue easy, and you are right. The right way to go easy is to forget the right way, and to forget that it is easy. Otherwise, you might get discouraged when it's not so easy to have ease.

Ease—being at home in your body, in this life, in this place, in this time—is another word for welcoming things home to your heart, being willing to experience what is arising in this moment. Usually, we want to be sure the moment is doing what it is supposed to or what we'd like it to do before we are willing to have it. This is challenging. How can you be at ease when you are wondering, *Is it okay? Is it all right? Do I like this one? Can I be at ease with this?* You want to make sure before you are willing to be with it that it is a

---

3 Rumi, "The Guest House," *The Essential Rumi*, trans. Coleman Barks (New York: HarperCollins, 1997), 109.

moment you are willing to have. Of course, this cautious assessing of what a moment has to offer leaves one anxious and uneasy! So part of sitting upright in the middle of your life is having no defense. It's all coming at you, and you just let it. You sit with it.

My teacher Suzuki Roshi would say, "Sitting meditation is to practice being ready for anything." Being ready for anything is different than gearing yourself up to defend or to attack things as they come toward you. You sit, and you're ready for anything. Begin right, and you are easy.

Tasting the True Spirit
of the Grain

When I was the cook at Tassajara back in the sixties, when we were just starting up at Tassajara, we were sitting in our temporary zendo and began having meals together in the zendo for the first time. Before that, we had family-style meals at tables. At the family-style breakfasts, we would serve hot cereal and put out white sugar, brown sugar, and honey because some people didn't want to be eating sugar. *Sugar is bad for you.* There were a lot of students practicing Zen macrobiotics. "It's too yin," they would say. There were also people who didn't like honey, so we served molasses. You wouldn't want to deny anyone what they wanted. Everyone should have what he wants, right? That's the American way. Have it your way, the way you want it to be. "Watch what you want to watch when you want to watch it."

Then we had milk. Some people wanted milk with more fat, otherwise known as half-and-half. Some people wanted, for some reason, canned milk. This was before 2 percent milk and nonfat milk and almond milk and rice milk and soy milk and different flavors of all those different milks. We only had to deal with so much choice back then. This worked when we had communal tables. We had one setup of these different items for each table. When we started having meals in the zendo, servers would take pots of food and go down the row offering food. The server would bow to two people, put the pot down, offer food to each person, then stand, bow again, and move on.

The condiments were on a little tray that people passed down the row. If you had one set of condiments at the beginning of the row and ten people in the row, it took a long time to pass all these items down the row and for each person to get the milk of their choice or the sweetener of their choice. We found that we wanted to have one set of condiments for every three people. If there were forty-five people in the meditation hall, there were fifteen sets of condiments and about eight different dishes with each of the different condiments. We're talking one hundred and twenty or so little dishes. After breakfast, do we want to put those things away and clean all those dishes, or do we want to leave them out, or do you put plastic wrap over them or what? How shall we do this? In the kitchen we were baffled.

About the second or third morning we had done this, somebody came out to those of us serving the meal and said, "Suzuki Roshi would like to give a lecture. Please come into the meditation hall before you go to the kitchen to clean up and have your own breakfast."

Suzuki Roshi said, "I don't really understand you Americans. When you put so much milk and sugar on your cereal, how will you taste the true spirit of the grain? Why don't you taste the true nature of each moment instead of trying to make everything taste just the way you want it to? Why don't you taste your own true spirit? What, did you think you could add milk and sugar to each moment of your life to make it taste the way you want?"

Those of us who worked in the kitchen were overjoyed. This meant a hundred or more fewer condiment dishes. After that, we thought, *Why don't we just serve sesame salt?* Traditionally in Zen, sesame salt is served with the rice. We thought, *we'll serve sesame salt with the cereal.* Ever since, when we have cereal in the morning in the zendo, we have sesame salt. Sometimes we serve yogurt and fruit with the cereal, but the first bowl, known as the Buddha bowl, holds only the cereal. You are instructed to preserve its purity.

One April 1st, we put Sugar Smacks in the first bowl, milk in the second bowl, and sliced bananas in the third bowl. We gave everyone permission to mix it all up. About one-third of the people, being serious about macrobiotics, were outraged because it was way too yin and too much dairy, which causes mucus, and too much potassium in the bananas. You never quite know what is going to push people's buttons. But we knew *that* was going to push their buttons—it was April Fool's Day!

The time I didn't realize I was going to push their buttons was one day when the oatmeal was rather thick. As a cook, I wondered, *Is there some way to cook that would please everybody and make them happy so they wouldn't make forays into the kitchen to attack me?* On this day, a group of people came into the kitchen after breakfast asking, "How could you do this? Where did you go wrong in life? Didn't your mother explain this to you? In the morning, your digestion is just getting started. You want to have cereal that is well cooked and thin and easy to digest. If it's thick and you have to chew it, that's hard on your digestion. Don't you know that?"

If you made the cereal thinner, there was another group of people who said, "We are working really hard. It's cold and wet, and we need fuel because we're working outside in the cold digging a septic tank by hand with a pick and a shovel and buckets. We don't get any meat. The least you could do is make some thick oatmeal, something we can sink our teeth into and chew."

I thought, *Okay. Let's put some raisins in the oatmeal.*

That's when the macrobiotics came in, "You're poisoning everybody. How can you do this?"

"Raisins? Poison?"

Not only is there no way to please everyone as the cook—how much do you think the world or anybody is trying to please you? In meditation we are aiming to receive the moment. It's clearly true that every moment is not to your taste. When there are some moments that are not to your taste or to your liking, what will you do?

This is Buddhist truth: there is no way to get moment after moment to be according to your taste. It's not your fault. It can't be done. It's not because of your lack of skill or lack of trying or lack of savvy or competence or your lack of self-esteem. It's not your fault that you can't get this moment or the next moment to be to your liking. That's the First Noble Truth. It can't be done. Not even enlightenment will help you have everything according to your taste.

So go ahead and taste the truth of the moment, the true spirit of the grain, the true nature of sadness or sorrow, the true nature of grief, the true nature of being, the true nature of joy, of pleasure, of happiness, of delight, of love. Go ahead and taste it and let the taste come home to your heart and digest it. Take it in and digest what you are eating, what you are experiencing.

Obviously, there are some things you don't want to take in and taste and eat. There are mushrooms that are poisonous.

There are experiences to avoid. But if you spend all your life trying to get the moment to be just right and just to your taste, you will overdo it. Pretty soon you won't be able to enjoy or savor much of anything because nothing is quite right. Eat widely so that you have the capacity to digest widely rather than having a narrow diet.

How do you develop the capacity to handle a wide range of experiences? Take in a wide range of experiences. In meditation, you're not moving, you're not talking, you have much less capacity to orchestrate the moment. More commonly you tell the moment, "Don't do that. Don't say that. Don't talk to me like that." Normally, through movement and talking and speech, you can orchestrate moments and make them more to your liking. How well has it worked?

You wouldn't be here meditating if it worked that well. You're here because you are learning to sit and eat, to take in the moment, however tasty or however pleasant or unpleasant, however it is. You're learning to taste and chew and digest. Your being will extract the nutritive essence, whether it's a pleasant or unpleasant experience, and you let go of the rest.

The idea in Chinese medicine and also in Zen is that the capacity to digest food is very closely related to your capacity to digest experience, to take in ideas, to take in emotions, to take things into your being and be able to absorb them and pass them through you. As you practice meditation, you will have a wide range of experiences. Some will be pleasant, unpleasant, happy, sad, joyful, painful, calm, upset. You will have a whole range of experiences, and you will grow from all of that.

So taste the true spirit of the grain. Let go of your endeavor to add cream, milk, sugar to each moment so it tastes the way you want it to. Learn how to taste things the way they are and be nourished by a wide-ranging diet.

GOMASHIO

2   cups brown sesame seeds
3   tablespoons sea salt

In a heavy skillet (cast iron is best), toast the salt until it turns gray. Set it aside.

Toast the sesame seeds, stirring constantly, until they start popping and turn a golden brown. Watch them closely or they will burn. Toward the end, you may find a lid useful to keep the seeds from popping out of the pan.

Add the salt back in to heat briefly with the seeds.

After cooling, grind the toasted seeds and salt with a mortar and pestle (or with an electric grinder) until the seeds crack open, releasing their oils. The gomashio will be light brown and sandy in texture—the seeds mostly crushed and rich with the aromas of sesame.

Store the gomashio in a tightly closed glass jar and keep it in a cool, dry place. It is typically served in a small bowl with a serving spoon.

Rotten Pickles

Suzuki Roshi once told us a story about the time he was a boy and went to study with Gyokujun So-on Roshi. There were a few young monks studying with this teacher. From him Suzuki Roshi got the name Crooked Cucumber. The teacher would tease him and say he was like a crooked cucumber. It was a term of endearment. Suzuki Roshi said that the other students were smart enough to leave but that he wasn't.

Each year the boys would pick daikon radishes, the large white radishes that are often twelve to fifteen inches long. We did this at Tassajara because, for a while, we were Americans trying to be good Japanese Zen students. We put the radishes in a big barrel with salt and rice bran (*nuka* in Japanese). The salt draws moisture out of the radishes and pickles them. The nutrients from the rice bran give the radishes flavor. We ended up with salted, flavored, pickled radishes. You can do this with carrots and Chinese cabbage and all kinds of ingredients to get different kinds of pickled foods. The traditional Japanese Zen breakfast is rice gruel and pickles. Don't get me wrong, I'm not recommending the Japanese Zen monastic diet. But we made these pickles at Tassajara.

Suzuki Roshi said that one year they made the pickles with Gyokujun So-on Roshi without enough salt in the barrel.

Instead of becoming salted and preserved, the pickles rotted. If you have ever been around these vegetables, you know they have quite the barnyard odor. You don't want to be in the vicinity of these radish pickles if they don't get pickled properly. Gyokujun So-on Roshi served the pickles anyway because in Zen we don't waste, we receive what is offered.

The young boys did not eat the pickles that were served. The teacher kept serving them, and the boys kept not eating them. Finally, after two or three days of this, young Suzuki Roshi decided to take matters into his own hands. In the dead of night, he took the pickles to the far end of the garden, dug a hole, and buried them.

This seems like a good aim with things that are distasteful. You find a hole somewhere inside yourself, put those things in there, cover them up, and endeavor to live your life so that you never have to go into that spot inside yourself again. It's called repression. Because you know where you hid these things, you know where not to go and you know how to walk and move so that area in your body doesn't get activated. You know how to sit so that you don't go into that area.

But if you keep sitting, eventually meditation will get into those places. Then the closet doors start to come open, and the places where stuff is hidden away start to open up. Your old memories start coming back to you. And you thought you were going to be doing this *spiritual* practice! Ah, well. You did not realize you would be cleaning out the basement.

So, back to Suzuki Roshi and the pickles. Sure enough, at the next meal the pickles were back on the table. His teacher didn't ask, "Who did this?" Instead, he said, "We are not eating anything else until we eat these pickles." Since we live in America, we find this story so wrong. Child abuse! They should have arrested him. But Gyokujun So-on Roshi didn't want to know who did it or have anyone confess to anything. He just said, "We are going to eat these pickles before we eat anything else."

Young Suzuki Roshi ate the pickles, and he said it was the first time in his life he experienced what in Zen is called *no thought*. If he had a single thought while eating those pickles, he wouldn't have been able to eat them. If you thought at all, you would spit them out. If you think, *This is horrible* or *I can't stand it*, you spit it out. You throw up. So he practiced *not thinking*. Chew and swallow. Chew and swallow.

Whether or not you have a mean and devious or child-tormenting Zen teacher, you are going to have experiences in your life that are "chew and swallow." There is just no way not to have those moments. Sometimes they are things you put off for years—ancient grief or sorrow. You put aside your old residual anger from your childhood or whatever it is, and the last thing you believe is going to occur is that you will have this painful experience you carefully stored away. But it comes, hopefully, at a time when you have the capacity to sit right in the middle of it and finally chew and swallow and be with what has been, up until then, so distasteful.

And strangely, you're nourished. Then you don't need to spend the rest of your life thinking, *How do I stay away from that? How do I get the others to help me not go there? How do I get the world to cooperate with me so I never have to be shamed again or humiliated or disappointed?* Finally, you have the disappointment you spent your life avoiding. And it's not so bad. You realize you can have this distasteful experience and go on with your life, and it's not the end of the world. Not having to avoid and manipulate, you find you have some stability and ease in your life.

There is something else. If you are not willing to taste what is distasteful, how are you going to taste what is pleasant and delicious and worth savoring? If you can't taste what is unpleasant, you'll have trouble tasting what is pleasant. You're so concerned about not having the experience (just in case it's unpleasant or painful) that you'll kind of have it and kind of not have it. Then, not fully alive in your life, you'll be letting life go through you, past you, and around you because it might be distasteful.

When you are willing to have the unpleasant and the painful, you can have delight and joy and energy and exuberance, vitality and creativity, determination and intensity. You can have all these things in your life that you couldn't have when you were being careful to protect yourself from the possibility of unpleasantness.

I didn't dream this up. I'm with Rumi: Who came up with this idea? Why organize the universe like this?[4] You create things that are pleasant, but when you chase after them, you can't get them. You go to get it, and you end up in the pigsty. It just doesn't work out the way it's supposed to. And it's not your fault. What a relief!

---

4   This is a paraphrase of Rumi's poem "Why Organize a Universe This Way?" from *The Rumi Collection*, ed. Kabir Helminski (Boulder, CO: Shambhala, 2000), 34.

You Might As Well Dance

People often ask what to do when bad things happen.
I think of Soen Nakagawa Roshi, who was asked,
"Roshi, I am so discouraged. What should I do?"
He replied, "Encourage others."

I don't know about you, but lately I've been feeling like a fraud. Do you ever feel like a fraud? Maybe this has to do with having had the fortune or misfortune of being ordained a Zen priest. That's setting the bar pretty high—what a Zen priest should be like. Completely enlightened, right? A worthy enough aim.

Still, it's hard to consider myself a fraud when I'm here at the Green Gulch zendo with all of you. When I'm away from here, I can be a fraud. Then I show up here and put on my robes, my costume, and people invite me to lecture, and I sit up in front of everybody, and it looks like I must be a Zen teacher. Everybody here is so wonderful to me. One person after another is so genuine and so friendly and so welcoming and inviting. It's amazing.

So is it true that I'm a fraud, or is it true that I am a Zen teacher? And what difference does it make? You probably have something in your life you wonder about. Are you a good mother? A good father? A good son or daughter? Are you a good spouse? A successful human being? How about that one?

I'm going to read you a story that left me thinking when I finished reading it, *What a fraud. What a fraud I am. Here is the Zen teacher.* I read it in a copy of *The Sun* magazine in the section where readers write in. This time the subject was gratitude. The last story in this section particularly struck me. I noticed the writer was from Belgrade, Maine, and I thought, *I know people in Belgrade, Maine.* I looked at the name, and it was John Gawler, my ex-brother-in-law. John Gawler is a wonderful person I've known since 1970, when I got married and he came to my wedding at Tassajara.

About two years ago, John and his wife, Ellen, decided that before their three daughters left home following high school, they would drive around the country in a truck with a camper behind it. The five of them came to our house in California, parked in our driveway, and camped out. One day they came into our house, and all five played guitar, banjo, fiddle, cello, and they sang. I was ecstatic. That family felt so wholesome in California—kids from Maine who play folk music together as a family. One day they went to San Francisco and got out their fiddles and played in the park. They went "busking" so the kids would have spending money for their trip.

I have known John for more than thirty years now, and I had never heard this story:

As part of Project Troubadour, I traveled with three other New England folk musicians to the West African nation of Gambia to give forty free concerts up and down the Gambia River. We took passage on an old cargo boat bringing salt, lumber, oranges, and coconuts to the far reaches of the country. When the boat docked to unload cargo, we would scamper off, make contact with the village chief, and find a large tree under which to give a free concert.

The children would gather around first, curious to see who these strangely dressed people were, and then the grown-ups and the elders. We would play tunes like "Buffalo Gals, Won't You Come Out Tonight?," "Down by the Riverside," "Oh! Susanna," and "This Land Is Your Land." They all kicked up their heels and laughed and showed huge appreciation that we had come such a long way to visit them in their tiny African village.

While on board the boat, we met a remarkable woman from Sweden who was also traveling the river. Her name was Mary Lindberg, and each year she saved up her money and made a trip to the leper colony at Bansang to bring supplies to the lepers and their families, who lived there with them at the colony. Mary also had her own supply of potato white lightning, which she stored in glass canning jars and generously shared with us. Before long, we'd agreed to do a concert at the leper colony.

When our boat docked at Bansang, we struck up conversations through our interpreter and with the colony's residents. We decided to begin the concert at once. A large crowd assembled. There was electricity in the air.

Soon after we ripped into our first number, I noticed an old man with no hands or feet, only stumps, dragging himself toward us across the sand. He stood himself up in the center of the circle, looked right at us, and smiled with joy. And then he started to dance.

He moved like no other person I've ever seen, as if on stilts, moving his thin arms, turning his fine head up toward the light, spinning in circles. Tears streamed down my face to see someone so carefree, so happy. Elliot, our leader and guitar player, was so overcome with emotion that he put down his guitar and ran out to dance with the man. I will never forget the sight of the two of them twirling together.

The man with no hands or feet turned out to be the village chief. After the concert, he invited me to come and have a cigarette with him on a large rock in a field. I don't smoke, but I couldn't turn him down. Conversation was difficult, but passing the cigarette back and forth between my hands and his stumps was a communion of the highest sort. The chief's inner light shone out of his clear eyes like a beacon of truth, and in his tribal tongue, he kept thanking the Great Spirit for our visit, for his life, and for all the good things that had been given to him.[5]

Stunning, isn't it? I ask myself, *How could I possibly be happy dancing on stumps?*

It doesn't matter so much whether or not I am a fraud. I may as well dance—and smile and greet all of you. One might

---

5   John Gawler, "Gratitude," *The Sun*, issue 315, March 2002.

consider the lepers outcasts, and I was born an outcast right from the start. Being premature, I spent the first three weeks of my life in an incubator. It was 1945, and I don't think in those days they had volunteers coming into the hospital to hold premature babies the way I hear happens now. That's like being an outcast. That is not being welcomed into a family, into the family of humanity.

In some way, of course, we are all outcasts. In one way or another, by the time we are grown, we will usually feel we weren't quite loved enough or honored or appreciated. We didn't quite fit in. We tried to fit in. We worked at it. We learned how to do it as best we could—or we identified with being an outlier or a rebel.

The suffering in human life is so deep and so unacknowledged—the pain of having human life and wishing so deeply to be part of everything, connected, accepted, appreciated, and loved, loved unconditionally for who we are, not based on our performance of late, whether or not we are enlightened or liberated, whether or not we are smart or stupid or financially successful or whatever it is. We may begin to wonder what will allow us finally to accept ourselves, accept our lives, feel our inherent fundamental connection with everything, with one another.

Perhaps, surprisingly, pain or difficulty may be what connects us with one another. Robert Bly, in one of his poems, says, "What choice do we have but to go down? How can I be close to you if I'm not sad?"[6] When you do go down, as I have done a lot, it may feel embarrassing or perhaps shameful to be

---

6   Robert Bly, "The Camels," *Talking into the Ear of a Donkey: Poems* (New York: Norton, 2011), 78.

so sad, so hurt. Out in the world there's not a lot of tolerance or acceptance for our feeling the painful emotions inside.

So it's often a lonely undertaking to be where we are, who we are, rather than sensing that we need to cover over our inner life, to hide, perform, pretend.

Often we feel nobody really knows us, nobody really sees us. Yet somebody inside may be crying. The person who is crying doesn't go anywhere. Often he or she has been tied down and hidden away. Tenderly, you reach out and touch yourself inside. Meditation is to be where you are, to touch yourself, to receive yourself.

I appreciate the Zen teacher Deshan, who said, "Realizing the mystery is nothing but breaking through to grasp an ordinary person's life." Please notice that this is not the same as having an amazing *samadhi* or being on the Buddhist freeway or cruising through somehow, immune, safe, and sound. There is no way to cruise through safe and sound, immune to life. If that is your aim, you won't be successful. It will be its own kind of suffering. It's one thing to reach out and touch someone who is crying. What about also reaching out and touching the person who is tying you down?

Suzuki Roshi said, many times, that *shikantaza* (single-minded meditation) is just to be yourself. Zen is to be yourself always, moment after moment. We are all those people. We are outcast lepers hobbling while dancing, yet overjoyed. We're tying ourselves down, and we're touching the pain. We're running away, and we are looking within. We're all these different people. Because we are all these different people, we know we're not just one of these people. We have freedom. We have choice.

Suzuki Roshi also called this "being true to yourself," so that you don't hide or run. He called it "not being fooled by anything, not being caught by something." This is also to be sincere.

Thank you for joining me in this great space where we can sit with our difficulty, with our pain, and accept our selves. We are human beings, and to be completely a human being is what we call being a Buddha. Thank you.

True Calm Is Not
What You Thought

In Buddhism, the general guidance is to
"turn the blame inward." But in the end, blame is not
helpful to yourself or others. You might find it helpful
to accept and appreciate your limitations.
And then be as present as you can in this moment.

I'd like to talk about the first line of the Heart Sutra: "Avalokiteshvara Bodhisattva, when practicing deeply prajna paramita, perceived that all five skandhas in their own being are empty and was saved from all suffering."

The Heart Sutra is called the Heart Sutra because it's the core or heart of the Perfection of Wisdom Sutras. *Prajna* is "wisdom," and *paramita* is often translated "perfection"— the perfection of wisdom. It is also known as "the wisdom that has gone beyond wisdom" or "the wisdom which carries you to the other shore." Perfection, or paramita, also takes you from this shore (so-called samsara, or suffering) to the other shore (nirvana, or peace).

We have to do something while we're alive. Rather than watching television, we Zen students chant and pass the sound of the Heart Sutra through our being, creating the sound, listening to the sound. It's cleansing to chant, to pass sound through you—the sound of your own voice and other voices, rather than the sound of the television or the movies or the traffic.

So chanting, passing the sound of the sutras through you, can be a wonderful practice. Sometimes people don't care for chanting, and they worry about what it means. Yet the point of chanting is not to worry about what it means, but instead, just to let the sound wash through you. It's cleansing. You let go of what is on your mind, anything you've been holding on to. While you are chanting, you let go of it. You are cleansed. Briefly, you let go of your thinking—that is, your preoccupation with getting somewhere.

I want to say a little bit about suffering in Buddhism. We'll start at the end of the sentence, "and was saved from all suffering," because I want to tell you in just a sentence or two what suffering is. We make one basic mistake, and once we make that mistake, we suffer. The one mistake we make is we identify the objects of our awareness with awareness itself.

If we see something beautiful, awareness is beautiful. If we see something ugly, awareness is ugly. If we hear a harsh sound, we think it's our mind. We confuse mind and the objects of mind. In that case, if we want to be calm, we think we need to make all the objects of awareness calm: *I need to get that sound to stop. I need to close my eyes so I don't see anything. I need to get my thoughts to shut up, and I need not to have any feeling happening, because if I have emotion going on, I can't be calm. In order to be calm, I have to control all these objects of awareness. I have to control what I'm seeing, what I'm hearing, what I'm smelling, what I'm tasting, what I'm thinking, what I'm feeling. I have to control all these things, and I have to get them to turn the volume way down or just be pleasant sights or sounds. Then I could be calm.*

Nothing to it. Except that in order to accomplish that, you will need to be guarded and alert so as to spot any infractions and make them stop. Busy making the disturbance cease and desist, you will not be calm. You'll be policing. So the basic mistake we make is to think that the way to be calm or peaceful or happy is to control the objects of our awareness, not only those of the external world but also our own thinking, our own feelings, our own sensations. Get those nicely under control, and get them to do what you'd like. Then you'll be happy.

How well has that worked? You've been doing it for twenty, thirty, sixty, eighty years. And has it worked out? Some of us take a lot of convincing. This is suffering: to try to control the objects of awareness. It's suffering because it can't be done. And attempting to accomplish this is inherently stressful. What will go wrong next?

We think, *My skill level is very low. Maybe if I practice Buddhism, I will have greater skill at controlling all these objects.* But it doesn't work like that. Instead, we end up having calmness to the extent that we stop identifying the objects of our awareness with *me* and *how I'm doing.* Though there's a loud sound, we could be calm. Though there's an emotion, we could be calm. Though there's thinking, we could be calm. We could be calm with whatever the object is because we are no longer identifying *me* with the object of my awareness. Does this make sense?

Of course it makes sense, but practicing it is something else. It is very tempting to control things. Things are out of control. They arise in an uncalled-for fashion. Do you ever have that experience? I have that experience a lot. I can be cooking, and I cut something, and then a few slices of celery fall on the floor. *Excuse me, but that was uncalled for. I wanted you to stay on the counter, all right? You didn't need to do that.*

Whether it's what somebody says or does or what you think or feel, things arise uncalled for and out of control. They don't particularly care what you want or don't want. Much as I've tried to develop my capacity for control over the years, it's not working out. I become more and more convinced to shift from control to compassion. With control, we're trying to get the object of our awareness to behave in the way that will make us happy or make us feel good about ourselves or reflect well on us. With compassion, we can appreciate the unique flavor of reality.

The first line of the Heart Sutra begins "Avalokiteshvara Bodhisattva." Avalokiteshvara is the bodhisattva of compassion. Often we believe that love means being able to control things. Believing this, we can become quite confused. When my daughter was little, she would fuss, and sometimes I would get frustrated: *I love you, so be quiet! Because I love you, you shouldn't be upset. I love you. Isn't that enough to make you feel better?* Of course my being upset with her would make her even more upset. She was way better at being upset than I was, so I would finally have to accept that my loving her did not make all the difference. More careful observation was necessary to find out what needed to be done.

Love, as is also the case with compassion, doesn't do anything. It's just with you. It allows crying. And love—compassion—doesn't abandon you. It doesn't run; it doesn't hide. Compassion stays and receives how you're feeling, what you're thinking. It's with you. Compassion is non-abandonment.

The bodhisattva of compassion is said to listen and hear the cries and whispers of all beings and to appear in just the fashion that beings are happy to meet. Compassion is not helpful in the way we usually think of something helpful. On the other hand, it's completely helpful because you have complete permission to experience whatever is going on in your life and not have to control the object of your awareness. You no longer have to control your feelings or your thoughts. Your awareness is compassionate enough to stay with you, be with you. It doesn't distance you or push you away or reject you or tell you to be other than you are. What a relief! Because you sense permission to feel your feelings, you are no longer compelled to act them out. Compassion is putting an end to suffering.

You can see how meditation is practicing compassion. If you sit still, you will start to experience many more things that are uncalled for. Everybody who has meditated notices that right away. *I was just going to find a nice place to be away from everything and get some peace and quiet, and all this stuff is going on. My knees are hurting. My thoughts are racing. I'm feeling frustrated. All these things are happening.*

So we're developing the capacity to experience and tolerate and be calm and peaceful with a much wider range of experience than we had before we started to meditate. Do we meditate or not? Meditation in that sense is not a quick fix. It's not like you have one insight that changes your life forever. But if you'd like, you could spend five or ten years seriously devoted to getting that one experience that will change everything. You'll learn a lot.

I did that for five or ten or twenty years. It's a nice thing to do, as good as anything. If you have the idea that one moment can change your life, go ahead and try. Give it your all. Convince yourself that you tried harder than anybody in history ever tried.

Most of the time, curiously enough, people sit in meditation, and after the period of meditation, they will say, "I didn't get anything." Yet the whole period of meditation is characterized by wisdom. Things are appearing and disappearing. You didn't get anything to keep, to have and hold on to. You weren't able to control your experience to anywhere near what is satisfying. You didn't attain a self that is lasting, that you get to keep and have. So every period of meditation is invariably characterized by wisdom, but we tend to reject the wisdom and say, "Why didn't I get something permanent, something lasting—some better capacity to control things and make a more beautiful self?"

It is useful to remind yourself that your experience moment after moment is always characterized by wisdom. What did you think? The big problem in Buddhism is considered to be ignorance: ignoring the wisdom that you already have. You overlook the three marks: suffering, impermanence, and no self.

In the early sutras, it is said you can go into a shop and see a bowl that would be nice for you to have, but unfortunately, when you look closely, it has three holes in it. It's going to leak. The three holes are the three marks. Looking closely, we always see these three. When we don't look closely, we like to think, "I could control things better. I'll be calm." As soon as you set out to do that, you have sabotaged yourself.

Now you will be even more agitated. You'll have to be on guard to make sure the things that arise in your awareness are calm. You'll try to get your thoughts to be calm and your feelings to be calm and your sensations to be calm and the people around you to be calm. *What will happen next? Can I sustain this? Can I keep it going?* Right away your efforts to maintain calm have activated a state of not calm. Calm disappears. When you want an experience to last, you are already fighting with the way things are: impermanent, without self, unsatisfying.

I've tried having one-day sittings at my house, in Fairfax in the little backyard meditation space outside the main house. Saturday morning is a big home-improvement day. Leaf blowers are going and the lawnmowers and the electric hedge trimmers and the chainsaws and the buzz saws. It's endless. How calm is that? *I wanted calm. I wanted quiet. I had my heart set on it.*

Once you have this insight, this wisdom, you can remind yourself to let the sound support you. Let the sound wash through you. You stop trying to establish a mind apart from the objects of mind. You stop trying to control the objects of mind. The world unfolds beyond your understanding.

This is the irony of our life. We don't understand. I keep missing the fact that as soon as I try to control things, I suffer. As soon as I try to have all these positive feelings and not others, peaceful thoughts and not others, and respectable images of myself, pictures of myself, and get others to agree with my pictures, I suffer.

I identify the objects of consciousness as being me. I identify them as mind itself. I forget that mind itself is not a thing; mind doesn't appear or disappear. You yourself do not appear or disappear. You are not a thing. You are Buddha. Buddha is not a thing. The things that arise in conjunction with your consciousness can be designated as tainted or pure, can be characterized as happy, sad, joyful, angry, frustrated, discouraged. This is something that arises in your awareness—not the awareness itself. It's not you yourself. It's a temporary designation. It doesn't have any lasting reality. It doesn't stain the mind itself.

If a sound arises, you hear the sound. If there's color in front of you, you see color. Mind does not discriminate. It is very compassionate. It receives what is going on. It doesn't say, "Don't be that way."

A skilled bodhisattva is said not to course in the skandhas, what's going on right now. He doesn't keep track of how well he is producing this and stopping that, of how calm he is or isn't. Because the skilled bodhisattva is not keeping track of how calm he is, he is calm. How calm it is not to be keeping track, not to feel that I need to keep track of how well I'm doing at producing and stopping various phenomena. I can allow my own response to life.

Dōgen says, "Let things come and abide in your heart. Let your heart return and abide in things." If you let your heart go out to things, you may not get it right, okay? You are shifting from control to compassion. You are shifting from approval to love. You are shifting from the head to the heart.

The Benefits of Meditation

I still sit each morning, even if briefly.
Even if you sit for just ten minutes, something happens.
A little awareness goes a long way.

As it is quite hot today, you might think you'd like to be at least a few degrees cooler. That's probably the first thing that comes to mind. If you let that go by—since we probably won't have much effect on the weather this evening—what's after that?

Is there anything just at this moment that you are wishing for or wanting? And beyond that? What is it you want deeply, intimately, perhaps even desperately? Or are you settled, at ease with this moment just as it is, not wanting anything in particular? Is that what you want—to be happy and at home in your own body and mind, settled in your own body and mind, settled in this moment, feeling all right about being here, feeling all right about who you are and what you are up to?

A monk once asked his Zen teacher, "What about people who leave the monastery after practicing for years and never return?"

"They're ungrateful asses."

"What about people who leave the monastery and come back?"

To this the teacher said, "They remember the benefits."

The monk then asks, "What are the benefits?"

The teacher says, "Heat in the summer. Cold in the winter." You thought there was something else to being here at Tassajara? You can get heat and cold anywhere. Sometimes we need to come to a place, either willingly or unwillingly, where we can appreciate the benefits of things as they are: heat in the summer, cold in the winter, being a human being.

So what is it you want? Second, what strategy are you using to get it? Third, is it working? Is your present strategy working? Is it an effective strategy? This is sometimes known as "view."

So we are talking about the first two stages of the Eightfold Path: view and intention. We're sorting out what would be a correct view and a correct intention without anyone telling you. You are figuring it out for yourself. A poem by Rilke speaks to this. I prefer Robert Bly's translation:

> You see, I want a lot.
> Perhaps I want everything:
> the darkness that comes with every infinite fall
> and shivering blaze of every step up.
>
> So many live on and want nothing,
> and are raised to the rank of prince
> by the slippery ease of their light judgments.
>
> But what you love to see are faces
> that do work and feel thirst.

You love most of all those who need you
as they need a crowbar or hoe.

You have not grown old, and it is not too late
to dive into your increasing depths
where life calmly gives out its own secret.[7]

7   Rainer Maria Rilke, *Selected Poems of Rainer Maria Rilke: A Translation from
    the German and Commentary*, trans. Robert Bly (New York: HarperCollins,
    1981), 27.

A Misbehaving Egg

As my teacher Shunryu Suzuki used to say. "Every day
is a good day, but it doesn't mean you can't complain."

A while back I opened the refrigerator door—I was going to
have an egg for breakfast. On the door are little cubbyholes or
dips, where I reached for an egg to pull it out—only it didn't
come out. It was stuck in the door's cubbyhole. I thought, *If I
keep trying to pull on this egg, it's going to break.* I kept pulling
on it anyway, thinking, *I'll be careful how I pull on this egg and
it won't break. I'll be able to get it out.* I tried wiggling it. It
was really stuck in there. Wiggle, wiggle, wiggle. But it didn't
wiggle. Finally, it broke.

I immediately got annoyed. *Why are you doing this to me?*
The egg started to ooze down white and yellow, drooling out
of its shell and all over the shelf and the mayonnaise and the
soda and all the other stuff below. I saw that it was going to
drip down onto the stuff below, and then maybe down to the
shelf below that. I didn't know what to do. Do I run and get
a bowl? If I run and get something to catch the egg, it's going
to be drooling down while I'm gone. If I reach my hands out,
I'm going to have to stand here while it oozes downward.

40

That's what I did. I waited for the egg to stop drooling and yelled out to somebody in the other room, "Get me a bowl!" I got it cleaned up finally.

But I was really angry about what happened. I bring this up because it's an example of the ways in which we get angry. It has a lot to do with the kind of world we think we are in and whether we think there is an enemy outside the walls trying to get to us, which is what I was thinking at the time. I had this picture of the egg saying to the refrigerator door: *Just wait until he opens the door. He thinks I'm going to come out of the door. Actually, when he opens the door and reaches for me, I'm going to stick to you, and you're going to hold on to me real tight. He's going to try and try to get me loose, but you just hold on. This is going to be really great theater because eventually he's going to break me. Then he's going to throw a fit. It'll be really entertaining. He might scream or cry or raise a commotion. It'll be really fun to see what he does.*

With something like that—with eggs and refrigerators getting together to upset me—what chance do I have? I am thinking that things are conspiring to get me; otherwise, what's the point of getting angry at them? Why would I get angry unless I add some psychology to it? You can get angry at a person and think: *Don't you ever do that again, or I'm going to be angry with you just like I am now. You're going to be in for it. You watch what you do, and don't behave like this anymore.*

But the egg is already broken. Besides, it never had that idea in the first place. There is nothing I can do—whether I scream or yell or get depressed or cry or moan—no strategy I can adopt so that the egg won't pull that sort of stuff on me in the future. It's just going to do what it does. This is very frustrating, that I do not have more power over things.

41

We think people are different, but people aren't any different. They don't set out to inflict anger upon me. Yet I can get angry at them and think it's going to be an effective strategy so that they don't pull that stuff on me in the future. But does it work like that? Have you ever noticed that working? It simply doesn't. There is not enough anger in the whole universe.

In a very few instances, perhaps it does. For the majority of people, it's not much use. At some point, they laugh at you and look at you like you're crazy. People look at me like that.

When I got angry, what did I really want? Did I want to be angry like that? Was getting angry like that useful? Did it work? Will every egg in the future come out of the refrigerator door, or will I continue to be distressed by how things behave? And why am I so disturbed when things don't act quite the way I choose? Do I want to be that fragile? Do I want to be subject to emotional distress and emotional affliction?

Build a wall. Is that going to work? Probably not. Do things not get to you when you have a nice wall? Another problem with the wall, of course, is that you have anxiety and worry about keeping it up and keeping guard so that a dreaded phenomenon you don't like can't get in—a sound, a smell, a taste, a touch, a thought, a feeling. It is going to get in, and you won't like it. You might have to experience something you don't like, something you wouldn't choose to experience. Heaven forbid!

Is there any alternative? I'm pretty convinced there is no strategy for never having to experience something I wouldn't choose to experience—if I even had the choice. Still, I continue to study and occasionally find new tools for being less susceptible to upset.

I do find I want to be patient. I want to be able to experience things I don't like with some degree of calm and awareness. I want to be able to experience things that are upsetting and painful to me with some graciousness, some dignity, some calm. I want to be able to relate with things in a more positive way. And that wish can make an invaluable difference.

Rujing, the Great Road, and the Bandits of Dharma

Suzuki Roshi once told us, "If you are not feeling kind to your breath, that is not our practice." Meditation is a way to give yourself to yourself. Has it occurred to you that you may have been trying way too hard? Give it a rest, dear one. There is a poem by a Chinese Zen Master named Rujing, the teacher of Japanese Zen teacher Dōgen, who travelled to China to study and then returned to Japan. Here is the poem:

The Great Road

The great road has no gate.
It begins in your own mind.
The air has no marked trails,
Yet it finds a way to your nostrils
And becomes your breath.
Somehow we meet like tricksters or bandits of dharma.
Ah, the great house tumbles down.
The autumn wind swirls—

astonished maple leaves
fly and scatter.[8]

It is often easy to feel lost or confused or separate, unac-
ceptable, unapproved, or unlikable. The poem begins, "The
great road has no gate." The great road is the spiritual path.
The great way penetrates everywhere. How could it be contingent on practice or realization? Rujing says the great road has
no gate. There is no gate you have to go through. Rather you
could cultivate a kind of trust or confidence that even with all
the ups and downs, difficulties, and stress in our lives, we are
on the great road, the great way. Your life itself is the great road.

"It begins in your own mind."
It is not outside at all. There is no other road than the one
you create, the one you are living. No road that someone else
is going to set you on. You'll need to investigate carefully to
find your way out of this mess (if that's what it is). All our
lives, all the mistakes and confusion are like this. Twists and
turns on our unique path.

The air has no marked trails,
Yet it finds a way to your nostrils
And becomes your breath.

The word for "air" in Japanese is sometimes the same
word used for "sky" and is translated as "emptiness." The sky
has no marked trails. Emptiness has no marked paths. There
is no way for you to find how to get it right. If you're looking
for "it's good or it's bad," there is no way to find that.

---

8 Edward Espe Brown, verbal memory. Source unknown.

I get so frustrated sometimes in cooking classes. Maybe we are making a tomato sauce, and I put in some salt, and someone says, "How much salt did you put in?" I put salt in until I liked it—to my own taste, to what I like. Do you want to trust your own taste, your own tongue, or do you want to think that you are going to get it right by doing what I did? Please learn to trust your own senses.

You create the way. You create your life. No one else is going to create it. You will have to find your way, just as the sky finds its way to your nostrils and becomes your breath. We are each finding the way by some mysterious process. How do we find it? All the time we do this. It's very mysterious.

"Somehow we meet like tricksters or bandits of dharma." You are going to do some stealing. You are going to have to play some tricks here. If you just try to do what you're told and follow the rules to please Mom and Dad and get their approval—well, why hasn't it worked yet?

You may need to steal it. It is a kind of stealing to just give it to yourself. Whether you deserve it or not, it is a kind of trick that you could give your life to yourself and have it. You can take it; you can give it. Chinese Zen Master Yakusan said, "Awkward in a hundred ways, clumsy in a thousand, still I go on." This could be a lot of fun.

"Ah, the great house tumbles down." That's usually understood as the ego or all the structure you have created to try to succeed with all the rules and strategies. And it all falls down. You cannot keep it up. Then something else can come.

"The autumn wind swirls. Astonished maple leaves fly and scatter." In the spring, it is daffodils and spring winds and new rains and flowers blossoming. Things are happening far beyond our control. The structure that comes tumbling down is the structure of how we try to control everything.

In his poem "Moving Water," Rumi says, "Don't insist on going where you think you want to go. Ask the way to the spring." In another poem, "An Empty Garlic," Rumi says, "You miss the garden / because you want a small fig from a random tree / . . . Let yourself be silently drawn / by the stronger pull of what you really love."[9]

It is so refreshing now and again to appreciate the bonuses, the blessings, of being still and not working too hard or trying to do too much. We can give our ideas of gain, of getting somewhere, a rest.

When we are in that space, we can also touch our pain and difficulty with mindfulness, and rather than trying to hide, we can touch it. Then maybe we can be with who we are and settle down and accept our lives. From there we can share our good hearts with one another.

Often, we find that this is quite enough.

---

9 "An Empty Garlic," *The Essential Rumi*, 50–51.

Two Demons at the Door

I've been remembering a poem by Zen Master Hakuin, the most famous Japanese Zen teacher of the last five hundred years, who is said to have had six major and eighteen minor enlightenments. He is famous for the "sound of one hand clapping" koan.

One story about him involves a local girl who was pregnant. Her parents asked, "Who is the father?" But she didn't want to say.

Finally, she said, "Hakuin. It is Hakuin."

Her parents went to the monastery very irate. They confronted Hakuin, "Our daughter says you fathered this child of hers."

Hakuin answered, *"Ah so desu ka?"* (Is that so)?

The parents said, "Okay, it's your child, and you're going to have to take care of it."

Hakuin said, "Oh, is that right?" And he took the baby.

Six or eight months later, the parents came back and said, "Our daughter confessed it was not you."

Hakuin said, "Is that so?"

"We want the baby back," they said.

"Is that so? Okay," Hakuin answered.

This story is often considered to be emblematic of Zen good sense and spirit: *Is that so?* This is the poem by Hakuin that I want to share:

Outside a demon pushes at the door.
Inside another demon won't let it budge.
Fiercely battling with one another,
Sweat pours from head to toe.
Fighting on all through the night,
At last, in the morning light,
Laughter is everywhere:
They were friends from the start.[10]

This is the way it is with our psyche, and it relates to a Zen saying that the disease of mind is to set up one mind against another—one mind that thinks it knows what's what, which mind is which, and which mind needs to be eliminated. One mind (that we identify with) thinks the other mind has too much resistance or is too shy or too depressed or needs some improvement. The one demon sets himself up as the one in charge, but the other demon is not going to take it lying down. What are they going to do?

Now you may struggle all through the night. Finally, in the morning, maybe it's okay. You don't worry. You've forgotten what the battle was all about. Of course, one night in Hakuin's poem isn't necessarily "one night." It could be ten years of two demons fighting before they realize they were friends from the start.

I was also thinking about a poem by Derek Walcott that emphasizes the becoming friends part. It's called "Love After Love":

The time will come
when, with elation,
you will greet yourself arriving

---

10 Translation by Edward Espe Brown.

at your own door, in your own mirror,
and each will smile at the other's welcome
and say, sit here. Eat.
You will love again the stranger who was your self.
Give wine. Give bread. Give back your heart
to itself, to the stranger who has loved you
all your life, whom you have ignored
for another, who knows you by heart.
Take down the love letters from the bookshelf,
the photographs, the desperate notes,
peel your own image from the mirror.
Sit. Feast on your life.[11]

Sometimes it's the last thing you want to do—just to sit with yourself. Can't I get rid of him? Can't I straighten her out? Can't I get her or him to be the way I want? Finally, you give up and "greet yourself arriving / at your own door, in your own mirror" and smile.

This is to shift from living in your head to living from your heart. It's in the head where we get headstrong. Thinking can be like a demon pushing at the door while the other demon disagrees and pushes back. It's in the heart where they can be friends. It's in your body. It's in your very close experience of phenomena—becoming intimate with your breath, your seeing, your smelling, your thinking, your feeling, and knowing yourself intimately.

I am reminded that Zen Master Dōgen says the first thing is to have trust in Buddhism, to believe that your life already is inherently on the path, that all your confusion, wrong thinking,

11   Derek Walcott, *Collected Poems, 1948–1984* (New York: Farrar, Straus and Giroux, 1987), 328.

and mistakes are part of that path. Each of us creates the path of practice with our own life. Perhaps you have been astray, then you reassess and redirect your efforts. When you believe you need to straighten yourself out, you have two demons battling with each other: *My life isn't on the path. If it were on the path, I wouldn't have so many problems and difficulties. What's wrong with you?*

One of the things Zen teachers point out is that the difficulties and problems are the path. You'd think the path is where you don't have those difficulties and problems anymore. But the path is having exactly your difficulties, exactly your problems, and studying yourself. How can I be with this? How can I meet myself "with elation" at my own door, in my own mirror?

How about if I try smiling? Sit. Eat. Feast. "Give wine. Give bread. Give back your heart to itself." In meditation there's an opportunity to experience very closely, intimately, whatever is happening each moment, whether it's a sensation or thinking. With thinking, it's harder to experience it closely because you identify pretty quickly with your thoughts: *I need to straighten this out. I need to do something. I need to make this different or better.* You get captivated—your thinking gets captivated—by a particular goal. But even with thinking, you can experience it closely and intimately. With your breathing and your emotions, you study how to touch them with your awareness and meet them intimately. *Shin*, the Japanese word for mind, is also the word for heart.

When your head doesn't get in the way and your thinking doesn't create demons to fight, your heart can take in your life, and you can feel whole, become intimate with things, and "greet yourself arriving." After all, "They were friends from the start." When we're not so involved in our heads (the demon outside versus the demon inside) or with what needs to be done or how things need to be straightened out, we can receive things with our hearts and start to sense the inherent virtue or blessedness of creation. In Buddhism, it's called Buddha nature—our own life marked with blessedness, virtue, preciousness. This is about touching something closely, intimately. It's not something you do with your head. It's something you know because you touch it with your heart. You become intimate with yourself, with your experience.

Try telling that to the demons pushing on those two sides of the door. They don't always want to hear about this. They're going to push until they just can't push anymore. When they finally tire, after struggling through the night, their hearts light up: they were friends from the start.

As we grow and mature, Buddhism suggests learning to perceive things directly, without these demons fighting, and to begin to trust our own observations about what's what. Of course, you'll notice that you can't always make things come out the way you want. That's the First Noble Truth. Is it your fault? Is there something wrong with you? No, it's simply the truth of the way things are, and you can observe it for yourself.

You can start to trust your own observations, your own perception, and you can start to know what's what, who's who, how you get caught in your own thinking, your own emotions, and how you get caught by others. It's a lot of tiny pieces of work, over and over, but you begin to trust. You experience your own observations and perceptions closely enough to know they are sacred and precious. It's Buddha nature—your original face, your true nature.

"You will greet yourself arriving / at your own door, in your own mirror"—that kind of true nature. And each will smile at the other. "Sit here. Eat. / You will love again."

One of our other habits of mind goes like this: *If I can't control you, I will abandon you. If I can't get you to behave the way I want, I will distance you, leave, turn the other way.* We do this to ourselves too. We do it in relationships, and we do it with our own psyches. We say, *I want my mind to be a certain way, and if it's not, I'm out of here.* I abandon myself.

This is what Walcott addresses in his poem: "Give back your heart / to itself, to the stranger who has loved you / all your life, whom you have ignored / for another, who knows you by heart."

Sweetheart, we can say, *how is it for you? I feel sad seeing you like this. Let me sit with you if I may.* This is to shift away from, *If you're so dull and dead, I'm out of here. I'm not going to have anything to do with you. I'm not going to hang out with somebody so dull and dead.* We may say this to ourselves, you know. We may abandon ourselves.

To practice meditation is to practice non-abandonment. We no longer abandon the self who is not behaving the way we expect it to behave, the way we believe we have to be in order to be loved. "Two demons pushing at the door." Meditation is not abandoning; it is meeting again and again the person you weren't going to have anything to do with.

Many of us have children or we work with kids, so we understand something about not abandoning them and not abandoning people in various diminished states and conditions. As you practice meditation, you become willing to be with yourself under a variety of circumstances and to be with others under a variety of circumstances. You don't abandon yourself, and you don't abandon others.

That is saving all beings.

Offer What You
Have to Offer

We have been planting trees at Green Gulch Farm Zen Center on Arbor Day for many years. The annual event reminds me of a passage from one of Suzuki Roshi's talks: "I am one tree, and each one of you is a tree. You should stand up by yourself. When a tree stands up by itself, we call that tree a Buddha. In other words, when you practice zazen in its true sense, you are really Buddha. Sometimes we call it a tree, and sometimes we call it a Buddha. Buddha, tree, or you are many names of one Buddha."[12]

Whenever I come to Green Gulch, I believe this. But when I am not here and only imagine being here, I don't remember that you are all Buddhas, and I worry about not being good enough. I sometimes see a chiropractor who has little signs and aphorisms around her office. Her favorite Stephen Levine quotation is, "If we each told each other our deepest, darkest secrets, we would laugh uproariously at our lack of originality."

I think it's pretty common to worry, as I sometimes do, about not being good enough. When I teach, it seems like my mouth is working and words are coming out.

---

12 Shunryu Suzuki, "Ordinary Mind, Buddha Mind," *Not Always So: Practicing the True Spirit of Zen,* ed. Edward Espe Brown (New York: HarperCollins, 2003), 58.

But yesterday, no words were coming out. I go to use my mouth but nothing comes out. I start to worry that people will say, "Loser! Incompetent! We heard you were funny. Now you can't even say anything."

In my world, I rely on certain things that come back to me. One of them is an affirmation: I offer what I have to offer.

I think this is also what trees do: they offer what they have to offer and share what they have to share. Dōgen Zenji, referring to an old poem, says, "Blossoming is the old plum tree's offering."[13] Offer what you have to offer. It's simple and challenging for us. Share what you have to share.

It's difficult to do this in the modern world. Often our friends are not living right next door. We have to drive an hour or two to get together for dinner. During the twenty years I spent at Zen Center, my friends were next door. I walked across the path or the road, and there was somebody to say hello to or have tea with. It's sweet to have a community.

When I say this, I think about trees, which seem to have community. One of the things trees have to offer is habitat. Various creatures can live in trees. Where there are trees, there are usually birds. Trees offer shade and fruit and a home. They graciously share their wonderful height. Pavement doesn't offer habitat. Some people say you are more likely to notice the sky when there's a tree.

An old Chinese poem says that "The silence in the mountains is deepened by the song of the bird." I try to remember that when the cars are going by at my writing retreat on Tomales Bay—*just deepening the stillness*. I see a huge awning of a tree out one of my windows. Even when

---

13   Eihei Dōgen "Plum Blossoms-Baika," *Moon in a Dewdrop: Writings of Zen Master Dōgen,* ed. Kazuaki Tanahashi (New York: North Point Press, 1985), 115.

it hasn't budded yet, it's a magnificent being to have in my vicinity.

Cutting down trees is part of what has led to global warming. Before all those acres of trees and forests were turned into newsprint or cleared for farmland or grazing, they were turning carbon dioxide into oxygen. Forests have also been burned for a few years of raising cattle. Whole communities, entire habitats, are sacrificed for short-term gain. Trees do not behave like this.

I've been thinking about what I have to offer. Each of us has various things to offer, whether it's a talent or simply our kind-hearted attention. Sometimes we think it needs to be a skill. People with professions, such as doctors, lawyers, or therapists, have useful and important skills to offer. At one of our Zen Center graduate reunions, I wondered if we are graduates or Zen dropouts? We're not sure if anyone has succeeded at this Zen business yet. One graduate lives in Japan and is working to combat global warming. Some of our graduates have started humane farming associations here and in Europe. One of my old friends from Zen Center has become a hypnotherapist, and working with him has been extremely valuable.

One of the things I have been interested in studying is communication skills. Some people have pretty good communication. They seem to be able to listen and hear what you have to say. What a concept! And they are able to say things to you that are not off-putting and that don't cause you to be defensive or to feel small and humiliated.

We have the capacity to be of service in various ways, such as planting trees. We cook for one another or garden, and we offer our efforts to benefit other people, plants, gardens, or the world. Some people are gifted at writing or playing music. Sometimes I think that if I have the chance in my next life, I'd like to be a musician. Making music seems so otherworldly and mysterious, yet engaging in present time.

Finally, our great offering is our own presence of mind and our own good-heartedness—our good-hearted presence that can enter this moment, show up here in this moment awake and alive, and be responsive to what is going on in our own being and around us. With our presence, we can show up and respond, and we can be awake and alive. Sometimes our offering will be like a tree in winter: it won't look like much. Other times there will be fruit and birds in the branches. Since our presence doesn't always look like much, it's easy to overlook our capacity to show up, to be present, awake, alive, and responsive.

The Japanese teachers at Zen Center used the expression *mei mitsu no kafu*, which they translated as "kind, considerate, compassionate attention to detail." I find this to be quite a profound teaching. With all the things I knock over and spill, I need to be practicing this more carefully.

One of my favorite poems is from Rilke's *The Sonnets to Orpheus*. I thought about this poem when someone mentioned planting sprouted apple seeds at Green Gulch Farm. Rilke's poem is about intimate presence, about showing up, observing, seeing, smelling, tasting, touching. Feeling is what actually connects us with ourselves, with one another, and with the world.

I used the following translation (mine and Hermann Clasen's, roughly) in my book *Tomato Blessings and Radish Teachings*:

Perfect apple, pear, and banana,
gooseberry . . . All of these speak
death and life into the mouth . . . I sense . . .
Read it in the face of a child
who is tasting them. This comes from far away.
Are names slowly disappearing in your mouth?
In place of words, discoveries are flowing out
of the flesh of the fruit, astonished to be free.

Dare to say what it is we call "apple."
This sweetness, compressed at first,
then, gently unfolded in your tasting

becomes clear, awake, and transparent,
double-meaninged, sunny, earthy, here—:
Oh, realizing, touching, joy—, immense![14]

For me, it's good-hearted presence that brings life to our own life, our own body and mind, and it brings life to the world, to apples, and to trees. As Suzuki Roshi says, "When you experience enlightenment, you will understand things more freely. You won't mind whatever people call you." I guess I have a ways to go.

Ordinary mind? We are all like this: ordinary mind and Buddha. When I am at Green Gulch Farm, I feel beneficent energy here in the meditation hall, our presence together, good-hearted people who have the capacity to be awake, alive, and responsive. And responding to things is different

---

14   Rainer Maria Rilke, *The Sonnets to Orpheus*. Version by Hermann Clasen and Edward Espe Brown, published in *Tomato Blessings and Radish Teachings* (New York: Riverhead, 1997), xix.

from controlling them or telling them how to behave. It's more like a tree providing habitat for birds and insects in its branches.

I want to encourage you to offer what you have to offer, regardless of what it appears to be or whether it appears to be valuable or not so valuable, skillful or not so skillful. This, finally, is the gift we can bring to the world: to offer what we have to offer, to share what we have to share, whether our skills, resources, or our good-hearted presence.

II

See What You Can Find Out

In the end, everything is practice.
Work is not just work. It is working on your self.
It is working on other people.

The Light in the Darkness

In Zen, we appreciate darkness. The sense is that when we try to live only in the light, we often find it upsetting to be in the dark, where we are much of the time. My Zen teacher Suzuki Roshi spoke of this, saying, "Zen is to feel your way along in the dark." When we have this sense of our life—feeling our way along in the dark—we're not in as much of a hurry, and we're pretty careful. We don't rush. We don't knock things over. We might bump into things, but we don't knock them over.

Little by little, we can find our way even though it's dark. When it's light and we know what we're doing, we often get in too much of a hurry and knock things over. We are not very sensitive. From that point of view, we could say, "Don't see darkness as dark. It's just dark." Or we could say, "Darkness is also light. There's light in the darkness."

I find the end of the year is difficult because I start to reflect. This year, especially, I feel kind of lost. I wish I knew what to do to make things turn out all right. Do you know that feeling? What's the recipe? I've spent a lifetime trying to make things turn out right. I thought Buddhism would help. But, of course, when you practice meditation, you find that it may not turn out all right but you can surrender to however it's turning out. And you reflect on how to respond to whatever has appeared.

I am reminded of basic Buddhism. Don't chase after the future. Don't dwell in the past. Live in the here and now. Here and now, in the present, we can have our awesome presence. I want to share a passage titled "Awesome Presence of Active Buddhas" from Zen teacher Dōgen: "Don't think that they're somewhere else. Buddhas invariably practice complete awesome presence. Thus they are active Buddhas." Please understand—that's us sitting, practicing awesome presence.

Michael Ventura tells this story about having lunch, or dinner, with Carlos Castaneda. A woman approached Castaneda and asked, "How can I have a spiritual practice? I have a good life, so what kind of spiritual practice can I have?" Castaneda answered, "When you go home, sit down in a chair, relax, and remind yourself that you and everyone you know is going to die, in no particular order. If you do this for a while, you will have a spiritual practice."

Maybe the circumstances of the world—the environment, politics, government—are now focusing us toward having a spiritual practice, an active practice.

The woman persisted with Castaneda, "How do I do that?"

This is how much we want some instruction. We don't have the sense that *this could come from me, this could come out of my life, out of my being. I will find my way in the dark, and I will allow myself to come up with what to do and how to practice. I will see what happens. I won't know ahead of time.* Wouldn't that be awesome?

"So," Castaneda answered the woman, "You give yourself a command."

That's pretty good, possibly even awesome. You could also give yourself a request, or you could make a vow, or you could acknowledge the vow that is inherent in your life or the wish that is fundamental to your being. You could acknowledge your wish for the kind of life you want for yourself.

Still, I'm trying to figure out how to make things come out the way they should, or the way I'd like them to. And they haven't. Why wouldn't I give it a rest?

In that same article by Michael Ventura, he wrote that Carlos Castaneda said, "For sorcerers, discipline is an art . . . the art of feeling awe."[15] We think, *If I were disciplined, I wouldn't have to experience pain. I would know how to get rid of it without having to experience it. I would know how to better defend myself from my difficulty.* It's an important shift, that we could actually have our life be awesome, both the difficulties and the blessings. We wouldn't have to defend ourselves from our difficulties or attack others for our difficulties and accuse them of being the cause. Blame can be a powerful habit, which inhibits our capacity to develop new skills for how to live.

Love is similar to awesome presence. We usually don't allow the experience of love to be here because we're so focused on approval, on measuring up, succeeding, accomplishing, deserving, and earning. Instead, we could simply agree to feel love. It's a decision, or a willingness. *I am willing to experience the love I've always wanted and dreamed about and never had, the love I felt I never deserved. I could let love be here.*

If you are willing to offer whatever you have to offer and receive whatever there is to receive, that's love. Love is something that flows. Love can be here whether there is difficulty or no difficulty. Suzuki Roshi talked about this occasionally.

---

15   Michael Ventura, "Homage to a Sorcerer," *Austin Chronicle*, July 28, 1998.

He said, "We practice meditation to purify our love." One of my aims for the coming year is to live in love, which isn't the same as not having any pain or difficulty. I am also aiming not to shame myself.

Why don't you just go ahead and change your world? Go ahead and empower yourself to live your life, to offer what is in your heart to offer, to imagine or dream or do with yourself whatever is out there? You may as well. What do you really want to do with your life, and what is the love, the gift, the offering you'd like to make with your time and effort and energy, with your self, your awesome presence? How will you manifest that?

I wish you a Happy New Year. Blessings.

Did I Create That Sky?

Did I create that sky? Yes, for, if it was
anything other than a conception in my mind
I wouldn't have said "Sky"—That is why I am the
golden eternity.[16]

JACK KEROUAC

---

16   Jack Kerouac, excerpted from *The Scripture of the Golden Eternity* (New York: Corinth Books, 1970).

Even a Thousand Sages
Can't Say

I have a couple of Zen stories to share. We'll see where they lead.

A student was sitting in meditation, and the teacher asked, "What are you doing?"

The student, who was Yakusan, answered, "I'm not doing anything."

His teacher then said, "If you're not doing anything, you are wasting your time."

Yakusan replied, "No. If I were doing something, then that would be wasting my time."

Then the teacher said, "Tell me something about what it is you are not doing. Tell me something about this."

And the student said, "Even ten thousand sages can't describe it."

I want to look at this question about doing, because for me, it's related to mindfulness. Mindfulness is not about doing. Mindfulness is just to be aware. You are not going to do anything about what you are aware of. You are aware of sound and taste and sight and emotions and feelings and pleasant and unpleasant and hindrances, and mindfulness doesn't do anything about any of that. Mindfulness is just awareness. It's not trying to fix, control, improve, or judge good or bad, right or wrong. With your awareness, you touch something. This is not doing.

If somebody said, "What are you doing in meditation?" you could say, "I'm doing mindfulness. I'm practicing mindfulness. I'm practicing just touching what arises in my experience moment after moment and letting it be." It is in this light that Yakusan said, "I'm not doing anything."

Doing covers a lot of things. People want to know how to quiet their minds. Do you want to be busy quieting your mind? That's a doing. Do you want to empty your mind? You could be doing that. Do you want to enlighten your mind? There are a lot of things you could be doing in meditation. We can get very busy. Sometimes we may sense that this "sweeping away the dust" is creating more dust.

I don't tell people to stop their thinking or to quiet their minds. When you try to quiet your mind, what happens? Every little thing that comes up—it's not quiet. Soon you have a big blanket over your mind trying to make it quiet. And the effort itself will be noisy: *I told you to be quiet! Now listen to me.*

There are a lot of things to do, but Yakusan said, "I'm not doing anything."

The teacher said, "Well, if you are not doing anything, you are wasting your time. You should be doing something. You shouldn't be sitting there wasting your time and idling away."

But Yakusan answered, "No. If I were doing something, that would be a waste of time."

I want to talk to you a bit about how "doing" is a waste of time. I like doing. I like to get things done. When I drive a car, I like to go some place. That's a perfect example of the problem with doing. If you are trying to go someplace when you're driving, everybody is in your way. As soon as you try to do something, you will have many hindrances, obstacles, resistances, and problems. If you're just sitting there in the car and going along with the traffic and not doing anything (like trying to get some place), nothing will be in the way. When I am aiming to get somewhere while driving, then a lot of people seem to be very Zen—either very Zen or very asleep. They don't seem to be trying to go anywhere at all. When the light changes from red to green, the cars seem to just sit there.

When you are busy doing something, you are not open anymore because you start to focus. You start to focus on *what I am doing*. The mind becomes limited when you get busy doing something. You just focus on *Am I getting it done or not getting it done?* You narrow your mind and check: *Am I doing that or not?* Everything else becomes irrelevant. You are no longer open to everything else. You make your mind small in order to do that one particular thing, and you don't notice everything else. Then you have success or failure around something you made up to do.

Suzuki Roshi said this as well. As soon as you try to do something, you make your mind limited. Why not have your mind be big? Small Mind decides to do this or that, or not to do one thing or another, to improve this or perfect that, or to have more of the better experiences and fewer of the less pleasant experiences. That's what we call Small Mind or monkey mind. It gets that all figured out. It's always busy.

When your mind is not so busy, then Big Mind has a chance to express itself. But you are not doing anything. Big Mind goes ahead and meets the world; it is one with the world already. And your life goes on. You're not stopping to ask, *Is it getting done? Am I getting things straightened out?*

If you are not doing anything, how do you describe this? When you are doing something, you can describe it. You can say what you are doing: "I'm standing up. I'm sitting down." But if you aren't doing anything, how do you describe that? In this case, Yakusan said, "Even ten thousand sages can't describe it." He could have said, "I'm letting my body leap." That would be a description of sorts—which would still leave you wondering.

With mindfulness, you touch each thing in your life. You touch and taste everything, and you don't have to worry about it much. Mindfulness has a tremendous power in your life because it makes it possible to actually own your own body and mind. To be mindful is to actually touch something. When you touch something, you can also let go of it. Often, we try to let go of things without touching them. That's called repression. If you try to let go of something without touching it—whether it's grief or sorrow or anger or shame or frustration—you store it some place in your body, some place in your being. *I'm not going to have that. I'm not going to touch it. I'm going to keep it at a distance from me.*

When we are busy not touching things, whether they are painful or pleasant, we may find ourselves feeling disconnected or unsettled—all from choosing not to touch what is there. We continue to feel isolated and separate and disconnected. The pain and suffering of life exists because we won't touch things. Yet it is a greater pain not to touch our wounds than to touch them. We think it would be painful to touch what is there in life, but often it is a greater pain not to. Of course, speaking practically, this may mean we need to work very hard to feel safe and secure enough to touch what is painful.

We work very hard, or we awaken the trust that we can dive beneath the surface.

In practice we cultivate the capacity to touch what is there, to hit the mark, to not make things up, to not try to be a perfect Zen student, to not try to perform everything beautifully, but instead to express ourselves in our lives, move through our activities, and see what comes up and touch it and be with it. This is the main healing in Buddhism: to touch things with an awareness that is compassionate and kind and warm. The compassion is that we are not trying to correct or fix. When we're aware of something, we don't make it wrong. When we are aware of something unpleasant in our lives—a sorrow or a pain—mostly out of habit, we think we must have done something wrong. Mindfulness is the capacity to just touch. And we all have it. The point of practice is not to create mindfulness but to strengthen it. Compassion is to listen deeply, to just receive so that you reveal yourself to yourself. You realize who you are, without deciding ahead of time who you should be.

Often parts of our lives become disconnected. We don't have to keep parts of ourselves separate from other parts. We can learn to touch them. There isn't one part of self saying, *I can't stand it. Don't be such a baby*—though I hear that one from time to time, *Don't be such a baby, Ed.* Can you imagine how you feel when you tell yourself that all the time? Do you think that makes you happy or sad? I can attest to the latter.

What are you going to do about it? Where will it end if you say to the voice that says, *Don't be such a baby*, "Stop talking to me like that!" At some point, you stop trying to stop it or start it or correct it or fix it. Mindfulness has the capacity to absorb everything. Mindfulness is actually you yourself, and even ten thousand sages cannot describe you.

Each of us is on the path. You have the path that is your life. I trust you to find your own way in your life. I want you to do that, and I trust you will.

The Gift of Attention

One of my first experiences of how powerful mindful attention can be was when I started sitting in 1965. I was meditating at the old Zen Center on Bush Street in San Francisco, in the former synagogue off Laguna Street. We met upstairs. Off the street we entered through big doors, then we climbed the stairs. At the top was a shoe rack, and to the left of that a door where we entered the meditation hall and bowed.

The first time I went there I didn't know what to do. I just walked in and did the best I could to follow what other people were doing. I went with my friend Alan Winter. Afterward, all the students lined up, and, one by one, we bowed to Suzuki Roshi in the back of the zendo, before leaving through his office and down a hallway back to the shoe rack.

I was quite concerned about what Suzuki Roshi would think of me. I was guessing he wouldn't think much of me because I didn't think much of me. Surprisingly, he didn't seem to think anything of me one way or another. It wasn't that he thought little of me; he just didn't seem to think anything of me. It was quite an unusual experience to feel so seen and so received, and yet it didn't matter to him what I was like. There was no indication of approving, disapproving, liking, disliking, or judging in any way, which was very refreshing.

He said, "Wait a minute," to me and to my friend Alan, and then he asked Katagiri Roshi to give us zazen instruction. Katagiri Roshi then led us back into the hall, and we received zazen instruction in five, maybe ten minutes: "Bow facing the cushion. Turn clockwise and bow away from the cushion. Sit down, turn around, cross your legs, lean from side to side, sit up straight, breathe. Don't worry about it. Okay, you're good." It wasn't much more than that.

Zen people are often like this: they don't give a lot of instructions. The expression in Zen is that if you give instructions, it's like gouging a wound in good flesh. We are all capable, intelligent people who can figure out things for ourselves. You have a mind and a body, and you can think and feel, so why wouldn't you be able to figure this out? Why would you limit yourself to doing what somebody else says when you could be trying out various things for yourself to see what happens? Why would you want to gouge a wound in your flesh, as though you were not capable of figuring things out? Traditionally, we try not to say too much. Katagiri Roshi did a pretty good job.

Both of the roshis used to say in their lectures, from time to time, "Zen is to settle the self on the self," and Suzuki Roshi especially would point first to his head and then to his abdomen. Move out of your head and into your body. Move out of your thinking and into your breathing.

So I began sitting. On Saturday mornings, we would have a period of sitting for forty minutes. Then we would stand in rows, bow and chant the Heart Sutra in Japanese three times. Following the chanting came breakfast, and after breakfast, there was a period of cleaning followed by two more sittings.

The cleaning was unusual too. The bell would ring for the period of cleaning, and we'd just start. This was the way these Zen people did it. Nobody was going to say, "You sweep. You mop. You wax. You do the bathrooms." You were to figure out for yourself what needed to be done and do it. Once Suzuki Roshi commented, "If you cannot find something to do, you are not a Zen student."

Zen also teaches that even people of high status do low-status jobs. So, though you may reach high status, you may still be cleaning the bathrooms. In fact, the head student or head monk, the *shuso* for a practice period, often cleans the public toilets. At Tassajara, their job is to clean the public toilets and empty the trash. Your high status does not exempt you from low-status activities.

When we clean the floor here, we sweep, but at the Zen Center, after sweeping we would take a wet towel wrapped around a piece of wood and run from one end of the room to the other bent over. It's like Downward Dog in yoga except that you're running while pushing a wet towel wrapped around a piece of wood all the way across the floor. I still remember, forty years later, Zen teacher Katagiri Roshi running bent over across the floor.

After cleaning, there were two more periods of sitting and then a lecture at ten o'clock. Those two periods were when I first realized that sitting could be painful. When you read about meditation, people don't say it hurts. They say, "Oh, you follow your breath. You empty your mind. You become still and calm." But your legs are killing you. When you read people's beautiful stories of their exquisite attainments, the stories do not mention how painful it is. I could sit for one period, but when I sat for two periods or three periods, it started to hurt, and I didn't know what to do.

As my legs began to hurt more and more, my breath became shorter and shorter. Default habits start to kick in: if you have pain, you move or do something; you get a Band-Aid or take appropriate steps. But when you are just sitting and get pain, what do you do? I didn't want to be one of those people who moved. I didn't want to fail at meditation. My idea was that you just suffer through and withstand it. To survive the pain, you grit your teeth, tighten your jaw, and then maybe you can withstand it. Then you start to breathe less and less. If possible, you hold your breath until it's over. As it turns out, you can't hold your breath that long, for thirty or forty minutes. You have to breathe, and then it hurts. As long as you're holding your breath, it hurts a little less. So I wasn't breathing very much, and my legs were hurting a lot.

Then I felt a hand on my knee. I knew the person sitting next to me was a woman named Jean Ross. Normally, in zazen, you don't touch anybody, and nobody touches you. She put her hand on my knee. Jean was the president of Zen Center, and she had studied Zen in Japan. I figured she knew what she was doing. I waited for her hand to pat me gently, as though saying, "There, there. It's okay." You know the way people stroke you: "It's all right. You're okay, little Eddie. Don't worry." I waited for her hand to give me some instructions. "Calm down. Let go." But her hand didn't do anything, didn't *say* anything. It was just there.

As soon as someone says, "There, there; relax," they are also saying, "What you are doing now is wrong, bad. That's not

what you're supposed to be doing. Why don't you calm down?"
As soon as some directive is given, you are making the person
wrong for not doing it that way in the first place.

What do you do with somebody who is having a difficult
time? Her hand was just there. My attention and awareness
shifted, and my breath started coming back to normal. My
body, which had been very tight and rigid, softened and softened and soon was nowhere to be found—only a warm glow
anchored by a sensation where hand met knee, though there
was no longer any hand or knee to be perceived. Not a trace
of pain. Calm, peaceful, round, vibrant—words being ten-
tative expressions for something ineffable.

After some time, the bell rang to end the period.

This being human is a guest house.
Every morning a new arrival.

A joy, a depression, a meanness,
some momentary awareness comes
as an unexpected visitor.

Welcome and entertain them all!
Even if they're a crowd of sorrows,
who violently sweep your house
empty of its furniture,
still, treat each guest honorably,
He may be clearing you out
for some new delight.

The dark thought, the shame, the malice,
meet them at the door laughing and invite them in.

Be grateful for whoever comes,
because each has been sent
as a guide from beyond.[17]

We have our habitual reactions to things. *I don't want to have anything to do with you. I'm not going to give in to you. I'm going to stand up to you.* My reaction had been to harden and resist and withstand pain, but simple, kind-hearted presence shifted everything. Then I was able to "welcome and entertain them all."

Instead of resisting and withstanding, I was showing up and actually meeting something, being with something while not being reactive. It was like meeting Suzuki Roshi. He didn't react. He met me. He acknowledged me, but he wasn't reacting one way or another: I like you; I don't like you; you're not like this; why don't you do that? He bowed—"treating each guest honorably"—and I softened.

Many years later, I read Zen Master Dōgen's teaching: "Supreme perfect enlightenment is like meeting somebody for the first time and not thinking about whether you like them or not."

We may begin to have these experiences in sitting as well: moments arise while we think nothing of them. When sitting, we might say, *I am going to establish a mind that is unperturbed. I am going to take my imperturbable mind and if pain comes up in my knee, I am not going to let that perturb me.* You soon discover that when you are so intent upon not being perturbed, holding on to your balance and stability so strongly, establishing it against all comers, your imperturbable mind

---

17   "The Guest House," *The Essential Rumi*, 109.

is bound to snap, and you will find yourself perturbed. To not be perturbed, is to not be perturbed. Whatever happens, it doesn't perturb you. Not because you are holding, but because you are softening.

This is an important shift for any of us. We start to have a sense of liberation or freedom because we can have experiences that don't perturb us anymore. To begin with, we feel a strong imperative to do something about what is painful, but we didn't know what to do. We didn't know how to be with what was disturbing. Perhaps our previous response had been to eat, stuffing ourselves with food, or to grit our teeth. We had a habitual way of not relating to something upsetting, but now, instead of not relating, we decide to be with it, to see what we can find out. Presence of mind realizes that choice is possible.

To consciously give your attention to something can be a precious gift. We don't always realize it, but when we sit and meditate, we are giving our attention to our own experience. We are giving attention to ourselves. We give attention to what is going on with our breath, our thinking, our feelings, our sensations. We're not necessarily so busy with getting something done, making something happen, or with correcting ourselves.

This receptive attention is quite different from the attention I received from teachers at school, who seemed to be looking for what I was doing wrong and would say, "Sit down. Sit still. Put that book away."

The attention I am speaking of is more like when your baby is asleep and you think, *So adorable!* There is the possibility of kind attention, tender attention, warmhearted attention to what's going on in your being, and not being busy doing things, gaining things, performing, getting somewhere, improving yourself. You have a chance to give yourself this kind of receptive attention, not the kind of attention that comes along with *I'm going to spot what is wrong and fix it or point it out to you.* You shift from the attention that's finding out what's wrong to the attention that's interested and curious and sensing things.

This is a great gift we give to one another from time to time: *How are you?* Actually being interested and sharing time to meet and check in.

Finding What You
Really Want

Suzuki Roshi said, "Don't be fooled. Don't always believe
what you think. Find out for yourself."

When I look carefully, I realize that I would like greater intimacy. True intimacy turns out to be quite challenging as it makes space for two, two people, two truths. So much of what we think of as intimacy isn't really intimacy at all. We start to get close to someone or something and want the object, the person, or even our own body to behave the way we would like. It makes us feel good. It makes us comfortable. As long as the person does what we want, it's just fine. We sit and breathe, and as long as our breath is a nice breath, we say, *That's very good. I'm being intimate.*

But what about when the other person doesn't behave that way? What about when your breath or your body behaves in ways you find distressing? It may do all these strange things. Perhaps your body gets hot, and you feel afflicted with the heat. Now maybe it's not so good to be intimate with your own body. You can't tell it what to do. You can't tell a friend what to do. It comes back again to that question: What do

I want? Do I want my body and mind and other people and things and the weather to do what I say? Or do I want to become intimate with each thing—my body, my breath, the people, the weather, the sky? Do I want to be intimate with things the way they are? And not struggle with attempting to make them different, better, or more likable?

What do I want? We can adjust our intention. It's like dropping a stone in the water. It goes right to the bottom. What is most important here? Boom! You get settled very quickly. If you settle what your intention really is, you settle the situation. You settle yourself on your intention with some clarity. You are settled on your strategy and how you are with people and what your effort is: to be intimate, allowing the other to be as is, or to be so generous you don't ask for anything in return, or perhaps to have compassion for yourself and others.

It's not something you have to make up. *I should be compassionate. I should be kind. I should be generous.* It doesn't come out of your thinking. It doesn't come out of a *should*. Instead, you decide for yourself. You settle yourself on your intention. You clarify your intention over and over again. You look and see if it works. Is it happening? Is it working? Or am I trying to get something I don't really need?

I used to smoke. When you smoke, you inhale the smoke and air into your lungs, and then you let it out. You sigh. It's satisfying. Then I thought, *Why do I need a cigarette to do that?* If I just want to breathe a little easier, sigh a little bit, do I need a cigarette to do that? The curious thing about something like a cigarette is that it reduces your capacity to sigh on your own. You need a cigarette to sigh. Instead, you could explore your natural capacity to enjoy your breath without all that hot air and smoke. It can be quite liberating to be freed from that dependency.

Part of a poem by Rumi says: "You miss the garden,/ because you want a small fig from a random tree . . ./ Let yourself be silently drawn / by the stronger pull of what you really love."[18]

---

18   "An Empty Garlic," *The Essential Rumi*, 50–51.

Accepting Yourself Completely

I want to remind you once again how well you're doing. Not only are you above ground but you're also vertical. It's rather unusual and remarkable to sit in meditation or to spend a day in silence. I think we sometimes take for granted or forget how unusual it is to sit quietly, experiencing our experience, tasting and knowing, touching our lives. To sit in this way and to walk in this way and to spend the day quietly is to experience the self in ways we don't usually have the opportunity to do. It's rare to notice the moments of life in more detail, or to feel our feelings, or perhaps to notice how much the mind races, or to find that we are still and quiet. Often we're rather busy in our lives and not quite so aware. We don't typically touch or taste or experience so intimately.

Just so you know, whatever you experience today, this is awakening. This is realization. We may have various ideas about what we might attain or accomplish: a special experience we might have that would be particularly peaceful or quiet, brilliant or dazzling. And of course, from time to time, people have such experiences. And then what? Usually, you will want to repeat it. When it doesn't last, you wonder, *What's wrong with my practice now? Yesterday I had such a great experience.* Or maybe you try to tell everybody, "I've had this great experience. I expect you to bow to me from now on." What will a picturesque experience do for you—once it's over?

Any experience that can appear and that you can describe will also disappear. It will be one more experience in all the experiences that arise and disappear. It's not possible to have any experience that would make all the difference in your life from now on—though it's tempting to want to have the one experience that will make all the difference from now on. Often we think, *If I could get rid of my anger or my desire or sit more still or be more concentrated or be more settled, then I would get the experience that will make all the difference in my life from now on.*

Do you understand how difficult this is? Not only is it difficult—it's impossible. In other words, it's a kind of mistake to try to get these experiences that will make all the difference. I say "a kind of mistake" because in making this big effort, we begin utilizing resources from deep beneath the surface of our lives, which in itself is valuable.

In Dōgen's school of Zen, we encourage ourselves to practice actualizing the present moment closely, not in order to attain a special experience but to let the experience come home to our hearts. By letting our awareness be touched by our experience, we wake up, we are moved by things, and we begin to respond to things from our hearts.

I think the biggest burden in life is to not like ourselves. Why would we not like ourselves, not accept ourselves, our humanity? Why would we do that? We think that in order to like ourselves, in order to respect or love ourselves, we would have to improve a lot. If we could meditate better or if we didn't have so many problems, then we could like ourselves.

We think we need to improve a lot before we can like ourselves, and we forget that we could accept or appreciate someone who is quite sincere, with good intentions, with a good heart, who isn't perfect. We could accept ourselves.

Sitting and practicing meditation, moment after moment, we are also practicing accepting ourselves. Sometimes we have good practice of accepting ourselves. Sometimes we're not so good at it. We may even encourage ourselves to accept somebody who's not so good at accepting themselves.

Some Buddhist teachers will say, "You don't have to practice for ten or twenty or thirty years to accept yourself. You can have a slight smile for yourself or decide to accept yourself or forgive yourself or others any time. You could decide to just sit and be with yourself. You could decide to receive your breath and the light and the presence in the room with you."

These are not the usual instructions for meditation: Sit there and appreciate yourself; sit there and accept yourself. It's too hard. It's a big challenge, and most of us aren't ready. So instead we say, "Why don't you follow your breath? Sit up straight, and don't lean to the left or the right. Don't lean forward or back."

Why don't you just sit in the middle of your life? See what it's like here. Welcome yourself home.

When we sit together in a group, we're also giving support to one another. Together we create this presence, or state of being, and all of us can sit in the midst of it. Presence and awareness are two of the gifts we share.

There are many ways in which our lives are challenging. People in our lives become sick, and sometimes loved ones die. We would love to heal them or save them, yet we do not have the capacity to make all the difference. There's the challenge of relationships and where we live and work. It's not particularly easy being a human being. The American myth is that it will be easy. If it's not easy, something is wrong with you, or someone else—take your pick.

I mention this because the fact that life is difficult means we may look for help and want someone else to take care of it, to make it all work better, whether we look for a partner, or to our children or parents, or to our teachers, our spiritual teachers. Someone else will make the difference and make it all work better.

Zen emphasizes the notion that you can rely on yourself and trust yourself and that the difficulty of your life, when you respond to it, brings out your resourcefulness and your resilience. We have the understanding not to look outside, but to look within. I sometimes use the expression that my therapist friend George Lane would employ, "Help is not on the way."

Suzuki Roshi's expression was quite direct, "When you're dying, nothing will help you. Not even enlightenment will help, as you have no more moments to live."

So in this moment, realize yourself fully. Express yourself fully. Have the fullest experience of your life.

It's like getting married to yourself. Will you have this body and mind in sickness, in health, in difficulty, in success, in wealth, in poverty? Will you have this body? Will you have this mind? *Yes, I will. I will have this life. I will have this body. I will have this mind.* Then you don't need to look anywhere else for an answer, for a solution, for some way out. When you've accepted this body, this mind, this life, you find your way.

Just Go Ahead

"You are the boss," my teacher Suzuki Roshi used to say.
"You are the boss of your life."

Today I am going to tell you some unusual things—outside
the Zen box. I was reading an article on writing in *The New
Yorker* by Joan Didion.

Ernest Hemingway said that a young William Faulkner,
who was terribly frustrated with a work of his own, wrote
to him trying to figure out how to finish. Hemingway
wrote back, "There is only one thing to do with a novel,
and that is to go straight on through to the end of the
damned thing." This was before the many tragedies in
Hemingway's life, before several plane crashes and failed
marriages. At the time, he had enough energy to follow
through with his convictions and just go on when a situation seemed at its worst and most helpless.

This is not so different from the advice that Suzuki Roshi
would give. He once said, "A skilled swordsman should be
able to cut a fly off a friend's nose without harming the nose.
You might think this is dangerous or wonder whether you
have enough skill, but you just go ahead and do it."

We worry about our adequacy. Am I skillful enough? Am I good enough to do what I'm doing? It is so uncertain, and at some point, there's no help for it.

To find our way in life, we will have to—as both Hemingway and Suzuki Roshi suggested—have some strong conviction. We'll just have to go ahead. If you wait until you're good enough or you're skillful enough or until you are sure of yourself and are certain to get it right, it may never happen. At some point there's no help for it, and you just go ahead.

In her article, Didion also quoted Norman Mailer: "It's almost a question of one's metabolism. You begin, after all, from a standing start and have to accelerate up to a level of cerebration where the best words are coming in good order." And it isn't just writing. They are the details of zazen or cooking or walking or eating. You have no idea what you're going to say or what is going to happen. You are starting from a standing start, and then you let something come out. You can't write anything if you worry, *Will I write the right thing? Will it be good enough?*—it's called writer's block. Norman Mailer said all writing involves a minimum of ego. Writer's block, he said, is a failure of ego. The minimum ego, he said, is that you are convinced that what you are writing is how it happened.

Anyway, we have the tendency as human beings to want to do the right thing before we do anything, and Suzuki Roshi's suggestion is to simply have the conviction to go forward. Suzuki said you can go forward when you forget about yourself. His language is different from Mailer's, but they are talking about the same thing. Forgetting yourself is also understanding that you cannot control how others will experience you. You let them have the experience they have.

But when we keep track of how we are doing and what others think, that will make it all the more difficult.

You start from where you are standing still, and you accelerate yourself into activity—into hearing and seeing and acting—where things are coming along. But at the same time, there's no help for it. If you wait for *I'm inspired* or *I'm sure it's okay*, then your whole life may be spent waiting. And over time you may find that worse than going ahead.

Suzuki Roshi told us that everything is encouraging us to attain enlightenment: the mountains, the rivers, the earth and sky, teapots and compost. Everything is encouraging realization. In the midst of practice at Tassajara, we actually notice this on occasion and feel tremendous gratitude. We notice the trees, the garden, or the rocks. We sense the way people are caring for the space here, and we feel that encouragement. The rocks and the water and the sky are waiting for us to show up, and then they will awaken us and help us with practice.

When we are willing to be with things, when we allow things to touch us, we can have direct experience beyond good and bad, outside right and wrong. To close, I want to share a poem from Rumi.

Story Water

A story is like water
that you heat for your bath.

It takes messages between the fire
and your skin. It lets them meet,
and it cleans you!

Very few can sit down
in the middle of the fire itself
like a salamander or Abraham.
We need intermediaries.

A feeling of fullness comes,
but usually it takes some bread
to bring it.

Beauty surrounds us,
but usually we need to be walking
in a garden to know it.

The body itself is a screen
to shield and partially reveal
the light that's blazing
inside your presence.

Water, stories, the body,
all the things we do, are mediums
that hide and show what's hidden.

Study them,
and enjoy this being washed
with a secret we sometimes know,
and then not.[19]

19   "Story Water," *The Essential Rumi*, 171–172.

You will meet the "light that's blazing / inside your presence." Suzuki Roshi said, "With that awareness, you forget about yourself and go ahead to take care of each moment and to meet what's in front of you." And you see that everything is alive and always encouraging you. Thank you for your good-hearted efforts.

The Backward Step

People will tell you all kinds of things.
Do you believe them? Often they want you to agree with
their story, but is it true? And by agreeing, do you help?
Remember that you're fine just as you are.

I want to talk about Zen Master Dōgen's "Recommending Zazen to All People" (the "Fukanzazengi").[20] He suggests we stop chasing after words and pursuing speech or phrases as though our lack of understanding is the reason why things aren't coming out the way we'd like. He says, "You should stop searching for phrases and chasing after words. Take the backward step and turn the light inward. Your body-mind of itself will drop off and your original face will appear. If you want to attain just this, immediately practice just this."[21] Then he says, "Set aside all involvements and let the myriad things rest. Zazen is not thinking of good, not thinking of bad. It is not conscious endeavor. It is not introspection."[22]

---

20 "Fukanzazengi," also known by its English title "Recommending Zazen to All People," is an essay promoting the practice of zazen composed by the thirteenth-century Japanese Zen Master Eihei Dōgen.

21 *The Essential Dōgen: Writings of the Great Zen Master*, eds. Kazuaki Tanahashi and Peter Levitt (Boston: Shambhala, 2013), 5.

22 *The Essential Dōgen*, 11.

Why would you think and analyze and spend so much time seeking instructions? Perhaps you are seeking approval, thinking that if you did what was right, avoided what was wrong, maybe you could gain more approval. Approval may be important, but is that it? Is that what you really want?

This brings us to my next question for you: What are you aiming for in your life?

In Buddhism, one sense of suffering is that we're going about things in a confused way, so we're not clear about our aim or our intention. For example, if you confuse approval with love, you will have this kind of endless problem. This is because even with all your efforts, you'll never be able to earn enough approval to gain the love that you have always wanted. There's no possibility of ever producing enough correct behavior. You might garner approval or recognition, but love is missing, compassion is missing. At times this is extremely discouraging for us, so Dōgen's advice is to let go of the struggle and have faith that you belong here.

Many years ago at Tassajara, in the sixties, when I was cooking, I worked very hard. I worked so hard that finally I was in bed for three days—where I had a chance to think about why I was working so hard that I basically knocked myself out. Well, I wanted the food to be good. If you're looking for approval, you're only as good as your last meal, and your approval will go up and down and up and down, along with your ratings—and then people actually say to you, "Oh, I don't see how you'll ever be able to surpass this."

That's scary. So I thought, *Well, who cares if the food is good?* And I thought, *Well, then people would like me.* Do you think so? People just like good food. They'd like the good food to continue.

Often, people who perform really well are some of the loneliest people in the world. The better your performance is, the less people actually meet *you*. They come and tell you, "What a wonderful performance! Thank you." But as a performer, you feel very lonely, and you can get quite desperate for a relationship. So I thought, *Why would I want people to like me and approve of me anyway? Well, with enough approval, I might be convinced to like and approve of myself. If enough people like me, then maybe it will convince me that I am likable.*

So I'm suggesting today that you will never get enough evidence of other people's approval to persuade you to love yourself. You'll never be able to succeed at liking yourself by getting others to approve your behavior. At some point, you know you're doing this for others, and then you resent them for making you do all these things to get their approval—while all too often they seem to be withholding their approval!

How much are you going to be able to like yourself for abandoning yourself to that scheme? When did we decide that was the appropriate view? What kind of person are you? Take the backward step and turn the light inward, and your body-mind of itself will drop away. Your original face will appear. In my language, this is to shift out of striving for approval into the realm of love. This is to drop the thinking mind, to let go of assessing and judging, evaluating good enough and not good enough, and to be willing to be with the experience of the present moment—just be with it.

There's another line from Dōgen's "Fukanzazengi" that I would like to share with you: "The great way circulates freely. Why would practice or enlightenment be necessary?" How could it depend on practice or enlightenment?

It's just like saying, "Love circulates freely." How could it depend on your performance? How could it depend on your approval rating? And he continues, "The mirror is already completely free of dust. Why would you think it needs cleaning?" What efforts do you think are necessary to clean your mind? Consciousness itself was never tainted. Later he says, "However, if you're still wandering about in your head, you may miss the vital path of letting your body leap." If you're still wandering about in your head, chasing after words, instructions, directions, the way to get it right, how to be good, then you may miss the vital path of letting your body leap. This is our life.

Your real life has this kind of potential—a kind of liberation from seeking approval, striving for better performance—of giving yourself greater permission to find your way, to not know what you're doing and let your body leap, find a way, discover the next step to take.

While your head keeps trying to figure things out to gain more approval or recognition, your body already knows. Settling into the body, we let it leap. This is similar to Suzuki Roshi's understanding of precepts. He said if you try to observe the precepts, simply trying to get it right, you'll be breaking them. The positive way of the precepts, he says, is to express your true nature, or we could say to express your true heart. When you don't express your true nature clearly, you apologize.

If you're always busy figuring it out, making sure, how much can you be at ease? You can't really, because you have the stress of needing to perform impeccably. It doesn't mean that we don't actually experience improvement or difference or change in our lives. It's just that we're not aiming for performing better. We're letting go and turning light inward so that life can unfold in a larger way. This poem from Dōgen is in his "Tenzo Kyōkun" ("Instructions to the Cook"):

> Through one word, or seven words, or three times five,
> nothing can be depended upon.

You yourself can't be grasped by words. Each of us finally is beyond words, beyond judgment, beyond approval or disapproval. Though we may be characterized by any number of designations or categories, we are in essence consciousness itself.

> Through one word, or seven words, or three times five,
> even if you thoroughly investigate myriad forms
> nothing can be depended upon.
> Night advances, the moon glows and falls into the ocean.
> The black dragon jewel you have been
> searching for is everywhere.[23]

What we've been searching for is right here: love, compassion, self-acceptance, choice, not knowing. The black dragon jewel is everywhere. Receive what has always been yours.

---

23 *Moon in a Dewdrop*, 60.

Everything Is Coming
from Beyond

I'd like to start with a Zen poem by Hafiz. Of course, it's not
exactly a Zen poem since Hafiz was a Sufi, but I'm calling it
a Zen poem. It's called "Tripping Over Joy."

What is the difference
Between your experience of Existence
And that of a saint?

The saint knows
That the spiritual path
Is a sublime chess game with God

And that the Beloved
Has just made such a Fantastic Move

That the saint is now continually
Tripping over Joy
And bursting out in Laughter,
And saying, "I Surrender!"

Whereas, my dear,
I am afraid you still think
You have a thousand serious moves.[24]

I consider this poem a Zen poem because I don't know that there's a particularly clear understanding about what meditation practice is good for. Is this practice one of your thousand serious moves that you still have left to make? Or are you going to be sitting with the understanding that it's over, I'm lost, there's no help for me now? Do you surrender?

You are the person you are. Who did you think you were? Who did you think you were going to improve to be? Were you going to get better at something? Maybe you could relax a little and not worry about it too much. Then you might find a little humor in this fix we're in called life.

Still, with no more serious moves, Zen Master Dōgen says, "Easy does it." Get a pillow or *zafu* (meditation cushion). Get a little height to sit on. Don't try sitting on the floor. That's really hard. Your posture is going to get all slumped. Sit up. Have a cushion. Grow tall inside. He goes on to say put this leg here and that leg there and lean your body from side to side. Take two or three deep breaths. Settle into steady, immobile, upright sitting. Place your hands into the "cosmic mudra."[25]

Okay, now what? Suzuki Roshi said in one of his lectures, "You remind me of Sunday school last week. I was with the Sunday school kids, and I showed them how to sit.

---

24 Hafiz, "Tripping Over Joy," *I Heard God Laughing: Poems of Hope and Joy*, trans. Daniel Ladinsky (London: Penguin Books, 2006), 66.

25 The standard meditation posture for the hands in zazen—in this case, our Japanese teachers used the term "cosmic mudra." With palms facing upward the left hand is placed on top of the right, with the fingers atop the fingers, and the thumb tips are lightly touching, so that the hands form an oval shape.

One little girl got into this posture and then she said, "Now what? Now what?" Suzuki Roshi went on to say in his lecture, "I think you have the same question."

This is pivotal. What is your next move? Is there another move? What are you up to? Is there a game? What are you trying to win? Who are you trying to defeat? What would you get better at? What are you doing?

When Dōgen first wrote the "Fukanzazengi," he said, "If you have a thought, become aware of it and let it go. If you do this long enough, your mind will become quiet." Game on! Can you get your mind to be quiet? If you do this long enough and your mind becomes quiet, now what? Twenty years went by and Dōgen rewrote the "Fukanzazengi" and took that part out. He said instead, "Think not-thinking. What is not-thinking? Beyond thinking." Settle into steady immobile sitting. See what happens. Let it come to you from beyond. See what comes from beyond. There is nothing other than things that come from beyond. What's coming from beyond today?

Yet we think, *I have a thousand serious moves, and I will determine what's going to come next, and I will make sure it's something good. I will make sure it reflects well on my meditation and my practice as a Zen student, because I want some credit for this, and I want to know this and prove it to others so they can recognize me as a spiritual hero. Won't that be great? Maybe when I drive down the street, the traffic will pause.*

Dōgen says, "Let your experience come." Game over. Not game on. Game over. Stop fiddling. Stop trying to have a better experience and somehow get your mind to have the right experience and not the wrong one. Settle down and see what comes from beyond.

Physical Challenges

I started practicing Zen in 1965. Some time in 1966 or 1967 while I was sitting in *sesshin*, I began to shake—often side-to-side rotational movements, my head, my shoulders, my hips—and I couldn't get it to stop. If I relaxed, I would stop shaking, but I'd also fall asleep. And if I fell asleep, I would be hit with a big stick called the *kyōsaku*: Bam! Bam! *You need to wake up!* Bam! Bam! *Oh, I need to wake up.* Then I would start shaking again. If I wasn't shaking, I was falling asleep and getting hit. This was called Zen.

What do you do? Think! Not think! This went on and on and on. For a while, I could shake so much that the tatamis (straw mats) in the zendo would shake in my corner. The whole floor would shake. Other students were sitting in a continuous earthquake.

Most people didn't talk about it. You don't talk to people about this. It's shameful. Some people wanted to talk to me about it and say, "You shouldn't be doing that. You should sit still. Zen is sitting still, not moving like that. You could stop it if you wanted. You do that to get attention. That's why you shake. You want attention."

I'm still here, folks, in spite of all the people who knew better than I did what Zen is and what Zen isn't. Excuse me for saying so, but I persevered. I kept on practicing. I didn't know any better.

After two or three years, Suzuki Roshi said to me one day, "I should have stopped you when you started that. I didn't realize it would go on this long." I don't know what he would have done to stop it. I was given little advice or teaching. I just kept sitting because I was going to practice Zen. I kept trying to sit up straight and follow my breath. We were practicing counting the breath: as you exhale, one; next exhale, two. Sometimes I'd think, *One, two*. I'd count my breath and shake.

After a couple of years or more, we were in sesshin, and they had moved me to the last seat in the zendo, near the door. It was December. Every time that door opened, gusts of cold air came in. We had these thin gray robes. As the weather got colder and colder, we put on layers and layers underneath the gray robes, trying to get warm. But it was freezing when the gusts of cold air came in. Though the zendo was unheated, it would get a little warm from body heat and the kerosene lamps, but still I'd get the freezing gusts whenever the door opened.

I kept shaking. If I got quiet, I got hit. On the afternoon of the third day of sesshin, after the many hours and hours of sitting, there was finally a period where I was hit four times on each shoulder. Then we did ten minutes of *kinhin* (walking meditation), and when we sat down again, I put my knees up. I put my arms around my knees. I whispered, "I can't do this." In seconds, Kobun Chino, who was leading the sesshin, was there. He said, "Let's go outside."

The moment I got out the door, tears poured down my face. I said, "Kobun, I can't see."

Kobun said, "Don't worry. Just hold my hand. I'm taking you to your cabin."

I saw blue skies and bare branches through the tears that kept coming. I got to the door of my cabin, and as soon as I crossed that threshold, I really started crying. Crying and crying. Kobun got me to lie down on my bed, and I started sobbing. I make a distinction between crying and sobbing. When crying intensifies, it becomes sobbing, and beyond sobbing is what might be called bawling. When you bawl, you are not just crying, you're also screaming. I was lying on my bed, and Kobun said, "Ed, you're okay. It's all right. Don't worry."

My whole body was shaking and my arms and legs—they were not just shaking, but they were flapping. And Kobun kept saying it was okay: "Don't worry. It's fine. It's not a problem."

After about half an hour, the bell rang for the service before dinner. Kobun said, "Ed, I need to leave now. I'm going to service and dinner. You are going to be fine. Get some sleep."

Kobun and I never talked about it again. This is Zen—Japanese Zen. Things happen. You carry on. About thirty years later, I took the opportunity to thank him!

It was easier to sit after that. Animals shake to release trauma. Perhaps that's what I was doing. If you hold the trauma in, you clamp down on what's inside. You don't let anybody know you are in pain because they might not like you if you have pain, if you "need help."

Ideally, in Zen you could sit and let everything come from beyond. You're not in charge. You could have all kinds of feelings surface. But often we try to keep the painful feelings down. We are trying to be skillful at this game and not reveal to ourselves or other people that we might have problems. We might have pain. We might have residual trauma. But we keep that under wraps so people will like us. They will think we're good students if we can just sit.

I couldn't just sit. I began to think, *I could be doing this for the rest of my life.* But I was also wondering, *Why aren't more of you shaking? How do you do this sitting-still thing?* There were many people who were better Zen students than I was—people who could sit still.

One day I decided to find out what to do. Maybe I could find out what was going on if I didn't try to stop it. I was sitting, and instead of trying to stop the shaking, I allowed the movement to unfold. My body started moving in giant spirals of energy. I'd sit for a while, then start up again with these unusual movements. Suzuki Roshi came over to me and said, "Do kinhin."

I got up and did walking meditation. But I found this very confusing. Was I wrong to see what would happen if I didn't try to stop the movements? In all the time I had been sitting and shaking, he had never before suggested, "Do kinhin."

So I went to talk to Suzuki Roshi a little later that day. "Roshi, for years I've been trying to stop this movement. When I try to stop the movement, I shake. Today I thought, *What if I don't try to stop it? What will happen if I don't try to stop it? I'd like to find out about that.*"

He said, "I'm so glad you told me. You should always see what you can find out. It's wonderful that you decided to find out something about what's going on, what that energy is. Thank you for telling me. Please continue finding out."

Zazen is not organized around human agency. You sit and let meditation do you or, in the case of the shaking, undo you.

You sit down, you sit still, you grow tall inside, you are quiet. The energy you normally would be using to move and talk is accumulating inside.

At Tassajara in those days, we were doing four or five periods of meditation a day, plus sitting for the three meals. Energy builds up inside. Do you think you are going to tell it what to do? Who knows better how to be that energy—you or the energy? Who knows better how to breathe—you or the breath? If you try to tell your breath how to do it, your breath gets anxious and uptight. You let your breath figure it out. Be aware, but allow it to be as it is. The energy will start to move in channels where it's not used to moving. Why hasn't it been moving in those channels before? Those channels had some blockages.

We unconsciously learned to do this when we were babies, before we were consciously deciding things. *I'm going to find a way to keep that inside.* Clamp! As that clamped energy inside starts to move after a couple of years of sitting, you may feel fearful, scared, paranoid. Another year you may feel angry. Then sadness may come up or disappointment. You're doing some basement work. You're cleaning out the basement, so things are coming up.

Things start rising. It's not because you decide to have them come up. You allow them to surface and let them go, and gradually these channels inside become more and more open. Then you start to have more energy, vitality, exuberance, and joy.

If you open a faucet that hasn't been opened for a while, a bunch of crud comes out. This is the rust, the crud that's in the pipes that comes out. After a while, the water runs clear. This process is to be expected. You're going to have it when you sit and the spiritual energy is developing, growing inside you. It's going to move in new channels, and debris is going to surface.

Sometimes people decide, *I'm not going to get angry. It's not Buddhist to get angry.* But you learned this when you were little. Then you found a spiritual practice to back you up. Later, at some point, you got depressed. You didn't realize that was the price of not getting angry.

The energy that could be anger is not just about today. It's old stuff. You could let that surface in sitting, but you need to develop enough stability so that your core energy goes deep down into the ground and then up through the crown and you grow tall inside. You have stability on your cushion; you've leaned to the right and to the left. As Dōgen said, "Settle into steady, immobile, upright sitting." I didn't have enough stability for many years. But when you're in place, things can arise. Perhaps it's a mess; crud comes up. But over time, you start to feel lighter. It's amazing that it takes years to figure this out, years to allow the debris of a lifetime to be cleansed. But we're in it for the long haul.

See what you make of all this. You probably will need to sort things out for yourself anyway. Don't take anything I say too seriously. I appreciate that you've undertaken a path, a practice of seeing what you can find out.

This is "the mind that seeks the way—beginner's mind."

Informed by a Daffodil

My friend Sharon told me a story about a friend of hers who had been a nurse for the homeless in Boston and then retired and moved up to Maine. After not working for a couple of years, she got a job distributing medications at a maximum-security prison. In the spring, when it was daffodil season, she decided to take a daffodil with her to the prison. She put it on her med cart but was worried about this because prisons are pretty uptight places. She was worried about what the prison officers would think, what they would say to her. What could happen? *Well, they could fire me.*

She started down the row and stopped at the first cell. The inmate in the first cell said to her, "Is that a daffodil?"

She said, "Yes, it is."

He said, "Could I smell it?"

She passed him the daffodil, and he smelled it. After a bit, he handed it back to her.

Soon each prisoner down the row wanted to hold and smell the daffodil.

One prisoner said, "That smells so good. I've heard that lilacs smell good too. I've never smelled one. I hope I can smell lilacs some day."

She went down to the end of the row where a prison officer was standing. He said to her, "I had no idea these men were so sensitive and caring. I had no idea."

What reality are you living in?

What reality were they living in? Many people, perhaps most, think prisoners are insensitive, uncaring creatures who simply need to be punished. Really? How are we going to treat each other? What are we like? How do we talk to each other? We are all people who want to smell daffodils.

Sometimes we forget, and we get caught up in our reality. We think (mistakenly) it will be helpful to be violent to someone. We get caught up in that reality. We believe it is real. What do we do with such a vision of reality?

This is difficult to talk about with anyone who is really caught up in their own vision of reality. We hope the person in charge, our awareness itself, can relax a bit about their reality and start to notice how sensitive or caring the misbehaving person is—the frightened, scared person, who may love to smell flowers. We don't have to fix this person or beat them into submission. Then we start to have a sense of peace and harmony. We can even have an experience of well-being and happiness with one another and with ourselves.

I will be here with you.

Reaching out and touching a flower; smelling a flower.

III

Cooking Your Life

Just as in cooking, there is no recipe for your life.
You'll have to find out for yourself.
Study with your senses. As my teacher said,
"Like moving along carefully and feeling
your way ahead in the dark."
Then you can learn and be informed.

Giving and Receiving

Cooking is not merely a time-consuming means to an end, but is itself nourishment, healing, meditation. When I first started to cook, I asked my Zen teacher Suzuki Roshi if he had any advice for me. He said, "When you wash the rice, wash the rice. When you cut the carrots, cut the carrots. When you stir the soup, stir the soup."

"When you are cooking," he explained, "you are not just working on food. You are working on yourself; you are working on other people."

I never forgot his words. You are working on giving yourself to what you are doing, giving your heart, giving your hands, arms, eyes, ears, and your whole body to the endeavor. You work to make cooking a craft rather than a chore. You throw yourself into it. You work to become absorbed. The price is a full measure of devotion—devotion to seeing fresh greens and wilted ones, devotion to sorting out dirt from leaves of lettuce, the stone from the black beans.

Each activity is the center of the universe where things are no longer things. When things are not just things, they become animate—alive, friends, companions. You taste what you put into your mouth. You taste the true spirit of each ingredient.

When cooking, we share in the effort that sustains our lives; we share in the bountifulness of the world. Onions and potatoes, apples and lettuces are intimately interconnected with earth, sun, sky, and water. Giving and receiving, they do their best.

I learned about wilted spinach salads when working at Greens Restaurant in San Francisco, where we had a fine one with feta cheese, croutons, and Kalamata olives on the menu daily. Here's one of my simplified versions.

SPINACH SALAD [26]
(serves 4 to 6 people)

1	bunch of spinach
½	cup almonds
½	teaspoon cumin seeds
½	teaspoon coriander seeds
	Juice of a lime (about ¼ cup)
¼	teaspoon salt
2	tablespoons honey
1	good eating apple such as Fuji or Gala
1–2	cloves of garlic, minced
¼	cup olive oil

Cut off the base of the spinach and the tough stems from the leaves. Wash the leaves thoroughly and spin them dry. Cut the largest leaves into halves or thirds.

---

26 *The Complete Tassajara Cookbook*, 226.

Roast the almonds for 5 to 7 minutes in a 350° oven or pan-roast them on top of the stove until crunchy when chopped. Sliver the almonds with a sharp knife, or you can try to do this with a Cuisinart on the pulse setting so that they are not turned to powder.

To make the dressing, start by grinding the cumin and coriander seeds in an electric grinder. Combine them with the lime juice, minced garlic, salt, and honey.

Cut the apple into quarters and cut away the core. Slice the quarters into thin lengthwise pieces and toss them with the dressing.

Put the spinach into a bowl. Heat the olive oil in a small pan until it is nearly smoking. Pour over the spinach with one hand while using tongs to toss the spinach with the other. If the spinach is not sufficiently wilted to your taste, press clumps of it into the hot pan with the tongs.

Toss the spinach with the apples.

Check the seasoning.

Serve on a platter or plates and garnish with the almonds.

No Measuring Up

Now I take time
to peel potatoes, wash lettuce,
and boil beets, to scrub floors,
clean sinks, and empty trash.
Absorbed in the everyday,
I find time to unbind, unwind,

to invite the whole body, mind,
breath, thought, and wild impulse
to join, to bask in the task.
No time lost thinking
that somewhere else is better.
No time lost imagining
getting more elsewhere.
No way to tell this moment
does not measure up.
Hand me the spatula:
now is the time to taste what is.[27]

WINTER SQUASH SOUP WITH APPLE, CUMIN, AND CARDAMOM

(serves 4 to 6 people)

1–2	winter squash such as acorn, pumpkin, Perfection, Delicata (about 2 pounds)
1	teaspoon cumin seeds
¼	teaspoon cardamom seeds
1	yellow onion, sliced
1	tablespoon olive oil
2	cloves of garlic, minced
1	tablespoon fresh grated ginger (about 1 ounce)
1	apple, cored and sliced
4	cups of hot water
1	teaspoon lemon juice
	Salt

---

27   *The Complete Tassajara Cookbook*, 332.

Bake the winter squash for about an hour at 375°. Allow it to cool, and then open it, remove the seeds, and scoop out the flesh.

Grind the cumin and cardamom in an electric coffee mill used for grinding spices. Or mince by hand, or grind in a mortar and pestle.

Sauté the onion in olive oil for 2 to 3 minutes. Then add the garlic, ginger, cumin, and cardamom; continue cooking another 1 to 2 minutes.

Add the apple and 4 cups of hot water along with the squash, and cook for 10 minutes or so. When the apple is soft, purée with a hand blender or a Cuisinart.

Season with the lemon juice and salt to taste. Taste again and adjust.

Virtue and a Cook's Temperament

Meditation is not really something we accomplish or do. We try, in a certain sense, to get out of the way and let things happen. Nevertheless, in the Zen tradition there was a Zen master, Hyakujo, who said that a day of no work is a day of no eating. And this became basic in Zen. Also, the Zen tradition we practice at Tassajara, the City Center, and Green Gulch Farm has a strong Japanese influence, and as I think you are aware, the Japanese are quite industrious. So Zen has a flavor of being energetically vigorous.

I began cooking at Tassajara the last year that it was a resort. Starting out as a dishwasher, I'd also learned to bake bread. Halfway through that summer, one of the cooks quit, and the owners of Tassajara, Bob and Anna Beck, asked me if I would like the job. Yes, I wanted the job. I was excited, though I had no idea what I was in for.

As a dishwasher, I had been a mellow, calm, reasonable person. Two days later, I was yelling at people. So you can see this as a kind of spiritual work, right? How will you do a demanding, stressful job with patience and buoyant spirit? I persevered through that summer, successfully enough it seems that when the Zen Center purchased Tassajara that fall, they asked me to be the first head cook for the fledgling meditation community. With two years of sitting meditation practice and two and a half months of cooking, just twenty-one years old, I was soon in over my head.

Where's the best place to have your difficulty? Because wherever you go, there you are—the difficulty will probably be there. You find yourselves in circumstances that challenge your stability of mind, but it's not the circumstances finally that are challenging. Difficulty surfaces when your skills and resources do not yet measure up to the tasks you are undertaking. It's unlikely that you will be able to arrange your life so you don't have to experience your "cook's temperament." Cooking, though not the underlying problem, will bring your residual issues to the forefront.

They say the same thing about meditation, that it will give you many good problems. Our Japanese teachers used to tell me this at Zen Center when I had problems. They'd say, "And if you weren't meditating, you wouldn't have these problems—and you've got some really good problems there."

We say then, as a piece of advice, pick your difficulty. That is, pick a good place to have your difficulty. Don't try to pick your pleasure or your joy or to do what is wonderful or pleasurable for you. Instead, pick a good place to have your difficulties. Pick the people you want to have your difficulty with, because that's what's going to be there, right? And this is not usually the way we think about our work or our relationships.

When I got divorced, I finally decided I was likely to have the same problems wherever I went, but it might be more useful if I had them with somebody else. I wasn't trying to say I don't have problems, but maybe there would be a more useful place to have them. I always thought having problems in the meditation hall was pretty useful, but it did little to prepare me for life in the world.

When I left Zen Center, I had to start writing checks, and I had to get a car, and I hadn't been to supermarkets much for twenty years. It was overwhelming. There would be ten or fifteen feet of shelves of toilet paper. *Oh my god, what do I buy?* Then people told me I wasn't watching enough TV because that's how you find out what to buy. It was really hard. And suddenly I had to start paying bills and get a job. There is such pressure. It was really overwhelming for me. I didn't understand how people do it. I mean, how do we do that?

Anyway, while at Tassajara, I tried very hard to be a Zen cook. I noticed that, from my point of view, other people weren't working so hard at that. You ever notice that? *Hey, I'm doing my part, but the other people don't seem to be doing theirs.*

I went to talk to Suzuki Roshi about it. I said, "These people—they come to work late. They want to talk about the dreams they had the night before. They're washing lettuce, but they're talking, and their awareness is not in their hands. It seems to be coming out their mouths in words. Their hands seem to stop. They get dysfunctional in their hands, and then they take long bathroom breaks. What do I do with these people? I try to tell them, 'When you cut the carrots, cut the carrots, and when you stir the soup, stir the soup,' but they don't seem to care. What should I do?"

He seemed to listen very sympathetically. Though not speaking the words, he seemed to be saying, *Yes, it's hard. It's really hard working with people like that. I know. You can't get good help these days.* But then he paused. "Ed, if you want to see virtue, you'll have to have a calm mind."

And I thought to myself, *That's not what I asked you.* But I kept quiet and kept listening.

He went on talking, and after a while he said, "When you're working on food, you're not just working on food. You're working on yourself, and you're working on other people."

And, of course, it turns out that's truer than we think. It turns out that the food takes care of itself. The part that's difficult is what's going on with you, what's going on with you and the other people, how to work with yourself and all the other stuff that comes up, and how to work with the other people and all the stuff that comes up. How do you do that? I started trying to see virtue.

I wrote *The Tassajara Bread Book* in 1970. In 1985, Shambhala, the publisher, asked me to revise it. And I discovered fifteen years after the book was written that it was all written in Suzuki Roshi English. We had all learned to speak the way he did! The book said, "Put bread on board and knead with hands." I had left out all the articles and the pronouns. I hadn't noticed that. So when we revised the book, I put in all the articles and the pronouns. "Put *the* bread on *a* board and knead with *your* hands." Let's get this clear, right?

But *The Greens Cookbook* we worked on rigorously. I worked on Deborah Madison's recipes, and she worked on my recipes. Then we worked with a food editor for a month, going over every word in the book. When we sent it in to the publisher, we felt great.

We got the manuscript back from our editor at Bantam, and all these prim little labels were sticking out the side—all these pink press-and-apply tabs. Wherever we had said, "Cook the onions until they're translucent," the little note would say, "How long?" If we said, "Season to taste with vinegar," it would say, "How much?" So we went through the book: "Cook the onions until they are translucent—about two to four minutes." "Season to taste with vinegar—beginning with a quarter of a teaspoon or half a teaspoon."

But are you going to look at the clock, or experience the food?

In the pasta section, we had said, "Cook the vegetables until they're as tender as you like." The pink label said, "How long? How do we know?" If you don't know what you like, who's going to tell you? What do you say? You'd better develop a standardized pressure of your chewing so you can determine whether the vegetables are tender enough or you need to chew harder. What do you tell people?

But this is interesting because what makes a cook is being able to notice the differences and decide which differences make a difference. You make decisions based on your aesthetic—and your aesthetic can grow and change based on what you see, what you smell, what you taste. You make decisions that come out of your experience. You take responsibility.

This is different from the school of cooking that says do what I tell you and everything will be okay. You won't have to taste anything. You won't have to smell anything. You won't have to look at anything. You won't have to think about anything. You won't have to decide anything. Just do what we tell you, and you, too, can make masterpieces.

That's tempting. That's often what cookbooks are doing out there. Thousands of people are reading them because you won't have to actually look at anything, smell anything, taste anything. You can do what we tell you. It'll be a masterpiece. You won't have to worry or have any anxiety. No problem. Everything's going to come out perfect. Just do what we tell you.

And then you go to meditation, and what? Everything's going to come out great if you just practice? I don't think so. My teacher got cancer. Two of my teachers got cancer: Suzuki Roshi and Katagiri Roshi. They died, though they had meditated. Some people say, "Well, I guess they didn't really understand the dharma, did they? They got cancer."

Anyway, everything is not going to come out all right. And then, at some point, that's all right. What else is there?

Rather than aiming to produce masterpieces, I started trying to find out how to make cooks. You have to actually put people in the position of being the cook.

And sometimes we have to do things that others might not completely approve of—they'd say "bad manners." Before he died, my father told me a dream about South Dakota that he hadn't told my mother because it wouldn't have been good manners. It would have been bad manners because I have two mothers. My first mother died when I was three. My present mother is actually my adopted mother. So in my family, we never talked about South Dakota because that's where my first mother was from.

Anyway, he told me this story: "I was driving through South Dakota and I had to stop and pull into a gas station, but this wasn't a regular gas station. In this gas station, there were no pumps out front; you drove around to the back where there was a big parking lot. You parked there, and then you'd go to sleep. When you woke up, you'd have a new car. It would be all gassed up and all ready to go."

Interesting, isn't it? So for us to find out about things, sometimes we have to be temperamental cooks, and sometimes we have bad manners. And bad manners aren't just bad manners. It's where something's really going on in our life.

And we should be able to touch it and know it and bring it into our life.

Choosing vigor can be very powerful. It gives us deep energy, enthusiasm, joy, and vitality, and we can bring that into our life and into our activity, into our being and consciousness. Then we can be really alive.

ED'S CHINESE CABBAGE SALAD

This is one of my favorite dishes for making at home—year in, year out.

Cut Chinese (Napa) cabbage in quarters lengthwise, cut out the cores, and then cut the quarters crosswise. The idea is for the pieces to be about 3 inches long.

Then "hand fry" by massaging the cabbage with your hands and some sea salt, which will soften it. This should probably be done no more than an hour before it will be served.

For the dressing, use what you have to get sweet and sour. I often use lemon or lime with honey or even a dab of chutney. Add grated ginger to taste. Add some sliced oranges or avocado, as is handy.

Garnish with some toasted sesame seeds, pumpkin seeds, or sunflower seeds.

In Search of the Perfect Biscuit

When I first started cooking, I had a problem: I couldn't get my biscuits to come out the way they were supposed to. I'd follow the recipe and try variations, but nothing worked. I had in mind the perfect biscuit, and these just didn't measure up. They didn't come out right. Finally, I asked myself, *Right compared to what?* And I realized that I had childhood pictures.

Growing up, I had made two kinds of biscuits: one was from Bisquick and the other from Pillsbury. For the Bisquick biscuits, you added milk to the mix and then blobbed the dough in spoonfuls onto the pan. You didn't even need to roll them out. The biscuits from Pillsbury came in a cardboard can. You rapped the can on a corner of the counter and it popped open. Then you twisted the can open more, put the premade biscuits on a pan, and baked them.

I really liked those Pillsbury biscuits. Isn't that what biscuits should taste like? It's wonderful and amazing—the ideas we get about what biscuits should taste like or what a life should look like. Compared to what? Canned biscuits from Pillsbury? *Leave It to Beaver?* And then we often forget where the idea came from or that we even have the idea. These biscuits just aren't right.

Meanwhile, people who ate my failed biscuits could be extolling their virtues, eating one after another, but for me, they were not right. Finally, one day a shifting-into-place occurred, an awakening. *Not right compared to what? Oh, no! I've been trying to make canned Pillsbury biscuits!* Then that exquisite moment of actually tasting my biscuits without comparing them to some previously hidden standard: wheaty, flaky, buttery, sunny, earthy, here. Inconceivably delicious, incomparably alive, present, vibrant. In fact, much more satisfying than the biscuits of my memory.

Those moments when you realize your life-as-it-is is just fine—thank you!—can be so stunning and liberating. Only the insidious comparison to a commercially prepared, beautifully packaged product makes it seem insufficient. The effort to produce a life with no dirty bowls, no messy feelings, no depression, no anger is bound to fail. How endlessly frustrating!

Sometimes, when I would be cooking, my partner would ask if she could help. My response was often not pretty, neat, or presentable. The lid came right off, and I would blow it: "No!" How could an offer of assistance be so traumatic and irritating? Neither of us understood how my response could be so out of scale, so emotionally reactive. But I suppose it just depends on which biscuit you're trying to bake.

I couldn't understand for the longest time. While I was no longer trying to be the greatest chef ever, I realized that I was still trying to make myself into the "perfect grown-up man": competent, capable, and superbly skilled, performing every task without needing any help. Someone's asking, "Anything I can do?" implies that I need help, that I am somehow not competent, independent, and grown up enough to handle the cooking myself. Ironically, the desperate attachment to being the perfect grown-up meant becoming a moody, emotional infant with strange prickliness. "How could you think such a thing?" I would rage. "You've ruined my perfect biscuits. Now leave me alone!"

As a Zen student, one can spend years trying to make it look right, trying to cover the faults, conceal the messes. Everyone knew what the Bisquick Zen student looked like: calm, buoyant, cheerful, energetic, deep, profound. Our motto, as one of my friends says, was "looking good." We've all done it: tried to attain perfection, tried to look good as a husband, wife, or parent. "Yes, I have it together." "I'm not greedy or jealous or angry." Sometimes we blame the other. "You're the one who does those things, and if you wouldn't do them first, I wouldn't do them either." "You started it." "Don't peek behind my cover," we say, "and if you do, keep it to yourself."

"Well, to heck with it," I say. Wake up! How about savoring some good old home cooking—the biscuits of today?

FLAKY BISCUITS OF TODAY[28]
(12 to 16 biscuits)

1	cup unbleached white flour
1	cup whole wheat flour
3	teaspoons baking powder
	(beware of old baking powder; it loses potency)
	For extra-cakey biscuits, you can also add a teaspoon
	of baking soda
½	teaspoon salt
½	cup butter
2	eggs
½	cup milk or buttermilk or yogurt

---

28 Adapted from *The Tassajara Bread Book* (Berkeley, CA: Shambhala, 1970), 98.

Preheat the oven to 450°.

Combine the flours, baking powder, and salt.

Cut the butter into the dry ingredients with a pastry cutter or two knives, or picking up pieces of butter and flour, use the heel of one hand pushing out along the fingertips of the other to flatten out the butter—and repeat. You're aiming for a mixture resembling polenta or coarse corn meal.

Make a well in the center and add the eggs and milk. Beat the eggs and milk with a fork until you have a uniform consistency.

Then continue stirring with the fork, gradually incorporating the flour, until all is moistened.

On a floured board, knead the dough just enough to bring it together—not too much or the biscuits will lose their flakiness and become tough.

Roll the dough into a rectangle a half-inch thick. Fold into thirds. Turn the dough a quarter turn, and repeat rolling and folding. Then repeat once more.

Roll out the dough to a half-inch thickness. Cut into rounds with a floured cutter or glass.

Place on an ungreased sheet pan (not too close to one another because, expanding in the oven, they will then run into each other). Bake at 450° for 8 to 10 minutes, until the bottoms are lightly browned and the tops are slightly golden. This may require starting off at the bottom of the oven and shifting to the upper rack for the final five minutes. A spatula can be used to check the bottoms. Do not overbake, or the biscuits will be too dry.

Coffee Meditation

During the years I lived in a meditation center, I rushed through my morning coffee. After all, if I didn't drink it fast enough, I'd be late for meditation. It was important to get to meditation on time; otherwise, one had to endure the social stigma of being late (obviously lacking the proper spiritual motivation), as well as the boredom and frustration of having to wait outside the zendo to meditate until latecomers were admitted.

When I moved out of the center, I had to learn to live in the world. I had been institutionalized for nearly twenty years. Now I was out and about. What did it mean? There was no formal meditation hall in my home. I could set my meditation cushion in front of my home altar, or I could sit up in my bed and cover my knees with the blankets. There were no rules. Soon I stopped getting up at 3:30 a.m. Once I did awaken, I found that a hot shower, which had not really fit with the previous circumstances, was quite invigorating. Of course, getting more sleep also helped.

Then I was ready for coffee—hot, freshly brewed, exquisitely delicious coffee. Not coffee in a cold cup from an urn; not coffee made with lukewarm water out of a thermos; not coffee with cold milk, 2 percent milk, or nonfat milk—but coffee with heated half-and-half. Here was my opportunity to satisfy frustrated longings from countless mornings in my past. I would not have just any old coffee, but Peet's Garuda blend—a mixture of Indonesian beans—brewed with recently boiled water and served in a preheated cup.

Unfortunately, by the time I finished the coffee, I had been sitting around so long that it was time to get started on the day, but I hadn't done any meditation. With this heavenly beverage in hand, who needed to meditate?

The solution was obvious: bring the ceremoniously prepared coffee in the preheated cup to the meditation cushion. This would never have been allowed at the center or in any formal meditation hall I have visited, but in my own home, it was a no-brainer. Bring the coffee to the cushion—or was it the other way around?

I light the candle and offer incense. "Homage to the Perfection of Wisdom, the Lovely, the Holy," I say. "May all beings be happy, healthy, and free from suffering." I sit down on the cushion and place the coffee just past my right knee. I cross my legs and then put the cup right in front of my ankles. I sit without moving so I don't accidently spill the coffee. I straighten my posture and sip some coffee. I feel my weight settling onto the cushion, lengthen the back of my neck, and sip some coffee. Taste, enjoy, soften, release. I bring my awareness to my breath moving in, flowing out. If I lose track of my breath, I am reminded to take another sip of coffee—robust, hearty, grounding. Come back to the coffee. Come back to the breath.

A distraction? A thought? Sip of coffee. Enjoy the coffee. Enjoy the breath. Focus on the present moment. Remembering the words of a Vipassana teacher of mine:

"Wisdom in Buddhism is defined as the proper and efficacious use of caffeine."

I stabilize my intention. "Now as I drink this cup of coffee, I vow with all beings to awaken body, mind, and spirit to the true taste of the dharma. May all beings attain complete awakening at this very moment. As I visualize the whole world awakening, my mind expands into the vastness."

TEA AND GINGER MUFFINS[29]
(a dozen muffins)

1	cup unbleached white flour
1½	cups whole wheat flour
¼	teaspoon salt
2	teaspoons baking powder
½	teaspoon baking soda
2	eggs
1½	cups plain yogurt
½	cup honey
	Zest of one orange
⅓	cup melted butter or preferred oil
2	tablespoons fresh ginger, grated
	nutmeg, grated

Preheat the oven to 375°.

Combine the flours with the salt, baking powder, and soda.

---

29 Adapted from *The Complete Tassajara Cookbook*, 190.

In a separate bowl, mix together the egg, yogurt, honey, orange zest, melted butter, and ginger.

Pour the wet ingredients into the dry and mix with as few strokes as possible to blend. Twenty is usually about right. Overmixing will make the muffins tough. I use a rubber spatula for this so I can get the residual batter off the sides of the bowl.

Grease a muffin tin (unless you have a modern nonstick one), or put a paper muffin cup in each pocket. Spoon in the batter about three-fourths of the way to the top of the muffin cups.

Grate some nutmeg over the tops of the muffins.

Bake for about 30 minutes until the tops have rounded and cracked and the sides have browned. On a recent batch, I discovered once again that it is not a good idea to use the bottom rack of the oven, as the bottoms of the muffins will tend to blacken.

A Cook's Inspiration

Inspiration comes from the strangest places. Gazing at tea-pots on the shelf at Tassajara when I was cooking there, I would feel a close camaraderie. I, too, was like that—dented, discolored, drained. Yet as I looked, I would sense something else: quiet dignity, tremendous forgiveness, the willingness to go on.

Sweethearts, I would think, *if you can do it, I can too.* And so it goes.

> Whatever is done will not make a cucumber
> more of a cucumber or a radish more of a radish.
> Cucumber is cucumber, radish is radish.
> What is done may make a vegetable more suitable
> to some particular taste—that's the usual way,
> to see what taste we want. But why not
> ask the cucumber, why not ask the radish?
> What is the taste it would like to express?[30]

---

30 . Edward Espe Brown, *Tassajara Cooking* (Boston: Shambhala, 1986), 21.

SMOKED CHEESE, MUSHROOM, AND ONION QUICHE[31]

1   uncooked pie shell
1   onion, thinly sliced
    Dijon mustard
½   cup grated cheddar cheese
½   cup grated smoked Gouda (or other smoked cheese)
½   cup grated Parmesan, Asiago, or Romano
1   tablespoon butter
1   cup sliced mushrooms
1   clove garlic, minced (if you would like)
3   eggs (or 1 egg plus 3 egg whites)
½   cup milk plus ½ cup half-and-half
    Tabasco sauce (optional)

Preheat the oven to 425°.

Cook the onion in a little olive oil slowly, until nicely browned.

Spread the mustard generously on the uncooked pie shell.

Sprinkle the cheeses evenly over the mustard.

Melt the butter and sauté the mushrooms for a few minutes, adding the minced garlic (if using it) for another half minute.

Spread the cooked onion and mushrooms over the cheeses.

Beat the eggs in a bowl. Whisk in the milk, half-and-half, and a dash of Tabasco.

---

31   Adapted from *The Complete Tassajara Cookbook*, 410–411.

Pour the mixture over the vegetables and cheese. Bake for 15 minutes.

Lower the temperature to 350° and continue baking for another 25 to 30 minutes, until a knife inserted in the center comes out clean.

Remove from the oven and let stand at least 5 minutes before serving.

*For another variation, omit the onions and sauté 2 cups of chopped fresh spinach with the mushrooms.

Cook, offer yourself, hold nothing back.
Cooking is not like you anticipated.
What is happening is unheard of,
Never before experienced.
You cook. No mistakes.
This is the way today.
You might do it differently next time,
But you did it this way this time.[32]

---

32 Edward Espe Brown, in Barbara Stacy's "The Heart of Tassajara Cooking," *East West Journal*, April 1986.

A Place at the Table

One of the primary ways we connect with each other is by eating together. Much of our fundamental well-being comes from the basic reassurance that there is a place for us at the table. Here we are served and will serve others.

ROASTED VEGETABLE PLATTER[33]

1	yellow onion
2	carrots
2–3	potatoes
1	red pepper
2	stalks of celery
	Several cloves of garlic
1–2	tablespoons of olive oil
	Several pinches of salt
2–3	teaspoons of balsamic vinegar
	Chopped fresh parsley and thyme for garnish

---

33 Adapted from *The Complete Tassajara Cookbook*, 391.

For baking, it is a good idea to cut the vegetable pieces into fairly large-sized chunks since thin slices will dry out in baking.

Peel the onion and cut each half into 3 to 4 wedges.

Wash the carrots and cut them into sections about an inch-and-a-half long. If some sections are fat, cut them in half, or you can make inch-and-a-half long pieces using the "Chinese rolling cut."[34]

Cut each potato into quarters lengthwise; then cut each of these into three or four pieces crosswise.

Cut the pepper in half and core and remove seeds. Then cut each half into 6 or 8 pieces.

Bend back the wide end of the celery stalks so that when they break off, you can pull off some of the strings. Cut the celery stalks into 2-inch pieces.

Add 2 to 3 garlic cloves, leaving the peel on. You can add more cloves if your audience really likes garlic.

Place the cut vegetables in a bowl and toss to coat with the olive oil. Sprinkle on some salt as well. Line a baking sheet with parchment paper and spread out the vegetables. Bake at 375° for about 45 minutes. Basically, you can just leave them alone, but it is also enjoyable to check on them now and then, especially since they might need tossing and turning, depending on how your oven is treating them.

When tender, remove the vegetables to a casserole or serving platter. Toss with the balsamic vinegar and check the seasoning. Salt to taste.

---

34   See *The Complete Tassajara Cookbook*, 38.

Freshly ground black pepper would also be good. Then garnish the result with the fresh herbs.

I find a short grace before meals helps us in untold ways. We are eating life that is giving us life, and by devoting our awareness to the remarkable path it has taken to our table—"we should know how it comes to us" is part of the traditional Zen meal chant—each ingredient has occasion to be appreciated and honored for helping to nourish our bodies. My everyday grace goes like this:

We venerate the Three Treasures
And give thanks for this food,
The work of many people,
The offering of other forms of life.

May this food nourish us
Body, mind, and spirit.
May all beings be happy, healthy, and free from suffering.
Blessings. Bon appétit.
(Or when I am in Germany, *Guten appetit.*)

Trusting Your
Own Experience

These days many people think that butter and sugar are unhealthy. I still believe in old-fashioned desserts. Thoughts can rigidify into hard-and-fast rules, creating a regimen that doesn't leave much room for enjoyment and satisfaction. I would rather be flexible and keep finding out for myself what truly nourishes me and what doesn't.

Returning to my own experience and learning how various foods affect me is an engaging and absorbing activity, whereas trying to impose someone else's thinking or scientific findings on myself ends up being stultifying and at times demeaning.

PEACH OR NECTARINE CRISP[35]
(serves 6 to 8 people)

4–6	peaches or nectarines, depending on their size
	Juice and grated peel of one lemon
1	teaspoon cinnamon
½	teaspoon freshly grated nutmeg
¼	teaspoon mace

---

35 Adapted from *The Complete Tassajara Cookbook*, 494.

½ cup brown sugar (or ⅓ cup, to moderate sweetness)
1 cup whole wheat flour or some portion
  unbleached white flour
2–3 pinches of salt
½ cup unsalted sweet butter
  Whipped cream or ice cream for a topping
  (optional)

Preheat the oven to 375°.

Put the peaches into boiling water for 10 to 30 seconds to loosen their skins so that they may be easily peeled. The nectarines do not need peeling. Remove from the water, drain, peel, core, and cut into slices.

Toss with the lemon juice, lemon peel, the cinnamon, mace, and nutmeg.

Arrange in a buttered 9 x 13–inch baking pan.

Combine the sugar with the flour and salt.

Cut in the butter with a pastry cutter or two knives.

Distribute the topping over the fruit.

Bake for 35 to 40 minutes at 375° or until the fruit is fork tender.

Serve warm with a dollop of whipped cream or a small scoop of ice cream if you dare (to go against the current food rules).

ROSE-SCENTED SUGAR[36]

(4 to 6 cups)

This is an excellent "secret" addition to a fresh fruit dessert. The aroma of the rose is what makes the sugar what it is. I first came across this item at some cooking classes with master chefs of Szechwan. This is how I do it.

3–4 roses
4–6 cups of sugar

Find aromatic roses—a delightful assignment. Remove the petals. Layer the petals in a jar with the sugar. Cover and leave covered for 2 to 3 days or even longer. Check the aroma. The sugar will absorb much of the moisture of the fresh flower petals. However, if the jar remains closed, the flower petals will begin to rot. So after a few days, when the sugar is damp, remove the flower petals and cover the rose sugar jar. Or you may want to remove the sugar from the jar and spread it out to dry for a few hours or in a slow oven on parchment paper.

---

36 Adapted from *The Complete Tassajara Cookbook*, 494–495.

WARM SOFT CHOCOLATE CAKE[37]

(makes 4 hearty-sized individual cakes)

½	cup butter plus some for buttering of the molds
4	ounces bittersweet chocolate
2	eggs
2	egg yolks
¼	cup sugar
2	teaspoons flour plus more for dusting

In the top of a double boiler set over simmering water, heat the butter and chocolate together until the chocolate is almost melted.

While that's heating, beat together the eggs, yolks, and sugar with a whisk until well combined.

Beat together the melted chocolate and butter. It should be quite warm.

Slowly whisk the warm chocolate and butter into the beaten eggs, so that the eggs heat slowly. Beat in the flour until just combined. Butter and lightly flour 4-ounce molds, custard cups, or ramekins. Tap out the excess flour. I've also used ceramic soup bowls or wide-mouthed ceramic teacups for baking the cakes.

Divide the batter among the molds. At this point, you can refrigerate the desserts until you are ready to bake them, up to several hours. Bring them back to room temperature before baking. (I leave them out for an hour or two.)

---

37 Adapted from Mark Bittman's "Molten Chocolate Cake," accessed May 6, 2018, cooking.nytimes.com/recipes/1014719-molten-chocolate-cake. Thanks to Marjorie Walter for alerting me to this delight.

Preheat the oven to 450°. Bake the molds on a tray for 6 to 7 minutes. The center will be quite soft, but the sides will be set. Allow the tops to stay wet in the center.

Use a heat-resistant rubber spatula or a spoon to loosen the cake from the sides, and then invert each mold onto a plate and let it sit for about 10 seconds. Unmold by lifting one corner of the mold. The cake will fall onto the plate.

Serve immediately.

Note: to reach my preferred texture of cake to lava—in my oven, they take 8 to 9 minutes. I've made them with various types of chocolate, but Valrhona is especially nice—70 percent cocoa is about right or half 70 percent and half 85 percent. I try to use organic butter, eggs, and sugar.

Jean-Georges Vongerichten, who originated the recipe, recommends serving with vanilla or caramel ice cream, and they are good that way. But I've also enjoyed them with fresh raspberries, ginger ice cream, or a little crème anglaise scattered with lavender. (This note is from Marjorie, who shared the recipe with me.)

Honoring Leftovers

All food is precious. All things are precious.
I've saved thousands of plastic bags. Is there any merit?
Maybe not, but Zen Master Dōgen said, "Don't waste
a single grain of rice." And that is my teaching too.

My intention is to take care of things, including leftovers, so I take an interest in using what I have on hand. One of the things I originally made with leftovers was avgolemono, a classic Greek soup. If you're going to have rice in your soup, do you want to cook it up just for your soup, or take out your leftover rice that is already cooked and turn it into Greek lemon soup?

To prepare Greek lemon soup, you whip up eggs with lemon juice, then you whisk some of the hot soup into the eggs to warm them up, and then you whisk the egg mixture back in to the soup, and you have Greek lemon soup, with rice in it. Cooking up the rice just to have it in your soup would mean extra time and effort, so take the rice from the refrigerator and you have a fairly quick soup. It's not complicated.

Once I looked at a recipe for minestrone, and it said a half a cup of spaghetti and three-quarters of a cup of potatoes and a half a cup of red beans. There was quite a long list of ingredients, which looked to me like somebody cleared out the refrigerator. And yet the recipe in the book made it sound as though you were to take these ingredients fresh from the cupboard to make your soup—and you just don't do that.

People making minestrone soup over the centuries did not start with fresh ingredients. This soup is a way to use your leftovers. You have some onions and garlic and some thyme and oregano and maybe some tomato, and to bring it all together you have all of your leftover pastas, and you make sure they will fit in the spoon, so sometimes you have to chop up the leftovers so they fit in the spoon, and then you have a delicious soup.

And people say, "How did you do that? Can I have the recipe?"

As Dōgen advised: "Treat the food as though it was your own eyesight."

Beautiful Leftovers   MINESTRONE

One useful concept for the use of leftovers is minestrone soup—at least that's what I call it, not knowing any better. Rather than beginning from scratch, see what leftovers you have available in your refrigerator. With a bit of luck, minestrone is the soup for you. Or did you want to follow a recipe and start with nothing?

To give the soup some body and flavor, we'll sauté some onions and add some garlic, thyme, oregano, salt, and pepper to help bring it together. At serve-up, we'll need a side of grated Parmesan, Asiago, or other hard cheese—or another cheese of your choice, for goodness' sake, though if you use Gouda, you might want to rename your soup Dutch Minestrone.

To the sautéed onions, we'll add leftover wine, water, stock, tomato sauce, juice, or paste as needed for liquid and volume. Any leftover soups? Beans? Potato? Tomato? Vegetables? Add them after the wine, before the additional liquid. Even leftover salads are quite likely to work just fine. Salad dressing? Vinegar? Good seasoning—the tart or sour element—as long as you don't put in too much.

Inventory everything and assemble it on the kitchen table. Do a visual assessment. For instance, one important step is elimination: anything spoiled, anything truly beyond minestrone. There is not much though—perhaps curries or beets. We're making Italian, not Indian, minestrone, and not borscht.

Go for it. Know the total quantity you want to make so that you don't overdo it and create more leftovers.

Take a leftover collection for your soup pot. A couple of cautions. First, develop a sense for the amounts of each leftover. If you really want minestrone soup, you cannot add so many leftover carrots that you end up with carrot soup. Same for rice, chard, or kale. Not too much starch, vegetable, or spice.

Second, consider the size of the leftover ingredients to be added. Check that the pieces are small enough to end up on a spoon. Sometimes some additional cutting up will be needed.

Okay, the salad is a bit limp, or the broccoli is tired. Let's blend it! Not rocket science, but let's do think things through.

You might even have some thematic spice or seasoning plans for the soup. Above we had an Italian motif, but no reason to be limited. What about other soup motifs? Consider the possibilities:

MEXICAN SOUP

Base: tomatoes, beans, rice, corn

Onion and garlic

Chilies: dried red pepper; ancho chili powder; fresh
green (jalapeño or serrano); canned green, which
might be roasted, peeled, chipotle (Fresh chilies
are commonly used in uncooked dishes. Dried
chilies are used in cooked.)

Cumin seed

Oregano

Fresh cilantro

Salsa

INDIAN SOUP

Base: lentils, cabbage, potatoes

Curry, chutneys

Savory: black mustard, cumin, fennel, onion seed,
fenugreek

Curry powder: sweet with cinnamon, cardamom,
cloves

Cumin, coriander, mustard, turmeric (beautiful
orange!), garlic, ginger, nutmeg

Red chilies, green chilies

Cilantro (called coriander leaves in Indian cooking),
sometimes basil and mint

Chutneys: fruit, tamarind, raisins, mango

EAST ASIAN SOUP

Base: tofu cubes, mushrooms, rice, greens, onion
Soy sauce, miso
Sugar, honey, maple syrup
Vinegar: rice, red, white, apple, balsamic
Garlic
Ginger
Red pepper
Green onion
Dark sesame oil
Toasted sesame seeds

Dreaming of Pizza:
A Talk for Children

I thought I would introduce you to the bells we use at meditation. When the bell is struck, we meditate. When you hear the bell for meditation, you start listening.

One of the first things to do would be to stop talking, because if you are talking, it is hard to listen. When I hit the bell, I have to listen too. While we're listening, see what you notice. Meditation is to come home to yourself and to the world. So let's listen . . . *Ding! Ding! Ding!* [A pause]

You hear some sounds, and we are also listening to how we feel today. How do you feel today? Go inside and see how you feel? Ask yourself: *Do I feel calm, centered? Or do I feel restless or scared? How do I feel?* See if you can notice how you're feeling at this time. Just let yourself feel whatever comes up. We'll all be feeling something different. Let's see what we feel this time. [A few moments of quiet.]

Was that an earthquake?[38] Did you feel that? And now we're all laughing! So that felt like a surprise. A little surprise, wasn't it? Should we risk trying again? Okay, then let's try.

Ding!

---

38 This was the 3.1 magnitude earthquake centered 4 kilometers from Dublin, California, recorded at 11:19 a.m. on February 2, 2003.

One of the things you start noticing is the sensation of your breath. Do you notice your breath from time to time? Let's try it. Let's see if we can notice that.

Breath is interesting because it carries us along, and it's always there. There's an inhalation followed by an exhalation, which together support our life. Some of you are sitting by yourselves and others are sitting with your parents. Are you being held? How does that feel? Are you sitting up on your own? Do you feel your body?

You'll have many experiences. Life is like an adventure. Whatever happens is an experience. Something will happen, won't it? I'll hit the bell and we'll notice what happens. Let's notice.

Ding!

What did you notice?

Did you have thoughts? Sometimes we think, *I'm having a good time*, or *I'm not having a good time*. Or *this is fun*, or *this is stupid*.

What else? Can you tell what will happen next? It's pretty difficult, isn't it? Hard to know what will happen, isn't it? Are you worried? Yes? What might you worry about? It might not be fun, or it could be boring? Yes, it might. So let's see what happens next.

Ding!

What happened? I hear the bells, and I feel relieved. I'm still here. How was it? Lots of things can happen. Is there some way to be ready for whatever will happen? No, I guess not. Sometimes we try to make something we like happen next. Can we do that? How good are we at that? Not so good?

So since you can't know what will happen next, let's see if you can just enjoy your breath and find a way to be a good friend to yourself. Look and see. And then you try to be nice to that person, whoever you are. And you can tell yourself, *You're doing well.* Thank yourself for being you.

Can you say thank you for whatever comes? We can't quite put our order in. Pizza? You're thinking of pizza? Whatever comes, we'll see what it is and say thank you. You can imagine pizza . . . pizza . . . pizza . . . and see if it appears. Are you thinking pizza? Are you happy to be thinking about pizza? Are you saying thank you to yourself for dreaming of pizza?

Well, thank you for meditating with me. Whatever comes next, you can say, "I will find out what to do with it, and I will say thank you." Let's enjoy this beautiful day.

Thanksgiving and Gratitude

This week is Thanksgiving. So I'd like to talk about thanksgiving and gratitude in terms of a Buddhist understanding. I confess to being the kind of person who, for whatever reason, when someone says, "Good Morning," has to pause and consider it.

On one hand there is a lot to be thankful for, but on the other hand, things could be better. And maybe we ought to hold out for a little more and withhold our thanksgiving or gratitude until we get a little more out of the deal. But of course, one of the basic elements of Buddhist practice is to be grateful for small and smaller things.

A number of years ago, we were having a tea at Tassajara, and we had a question-and-answer period. A student asked, a little pointedly, "Suzuki Roshi, why haven't you enlightened me yet?" This is not a respectful question to ask your teacher. But on the other hand, it may be a bit like what parents do with their kids—or kids do with their folks: "What have you done for me lately?" or "Why can't you get it together?" We often accuse or challenge each other about various things. Sometimes it's not intended to be hurtful. People might say things like, "Why haven't you enlightened me yet?"

Suzuki Roshi was polite and kind in his response. He said, "I'm making my best effort." And he didn't say, "How about you?" or anything like that. He was very careful in his response. He said, "I'm making my best effort," and nothing more. He left it right there. Without judgment.

I don't think we acknowledge that each person is making their best effort, whether it is the teacher or the student, the parent or the child. Sometimes the student is trying pretty hard, and the teacher doesn't appreciate it, or the teacher may be working pretty hard to be supportive, and the student doesn't feel it.

When I told Suzuki Roshi, "I'm confused," or "I don't understand," he would sometimes say, "Oh, thank you for telling me." When there is a feeling of appreciation or gratitude, there is more of a sense of connection. If we put this kind of dialogue inside, the inner landscape softens. Sometimes, if my body is hurting, I'll tell it to shut up. I don't say, *Thank you for telling me you are tired*, or *Oh, you're scared. Tell me more about that.* On the one hand, if I get angry or I am upset and confused, and I listen very carefully, I can hear inside, *I'm making my best effort.* On the other hand, part of me might say, *That's not good enough. Why don't you give me some powerful, stunning experience that would make me feel really good? Why can't you do that?*

And in this fashion, we may tend to demean ourselves because we don't hear the sincerity and goodness of our own bodies and minds. We don't notice our body and mind are making their best effort, in spite of being tired.

There's an expression in Zen: If you want to attain intimacy, don't ask with a question. We aim to be careful, as there is a difference, for instance, between "How's it going?" and "Why are you like that?" or "What's wrong?"

How do we receive the world, and how do we appear in the world? And when we have thankfulness for receiving our experience, we also have gratitude for the way other people and things are making their best efforts. Then we have some resonance with the world. And this becomes the basis for imperturbability, because we can see and appreciate what is happening as part of Big Mind. And we know there is no way to control Big Mind. We can have some gratitude and thankfulness as we receive the experience of this moment.

One time a monk asked Zhaozhou, a Chinese Buddhist master, "To whom does the Buddha give passion?" Passion, in this sense, is a word to cover afflictive emotions such as greed, hate, lust—intense emotions that afflict us and other people. Yet passion is also a word that covers enthusiasm and drive, inspiration and aspiration.

"To whom does Buddha give passion?"

Zhaozhou said, "Buddha gives passion to everyone."

The monk said, "How do we get rid of it?"

And Zhaozhou said, "Why should we get rid of it?"

It's this way when we try to control our minds and bodies or someone else's. "You have to do something about that. I don't want that around here." This already sets up tension in a situation.

Suzuki Roshi used to call these mind waves or mind weeds. There are many mind weeds, and when you don't understand how to turn the weeds into compost, you can make a lot of mistakes. If you can find out how to use the weeds properly, you can nourish your garden, but if you only try to get rid of the weeds, pretty soon you are just destroying the whole garden. Everything starts to look like a weed. There is no beauty left.

On the other hand, afflictive emotions can be transformed into positive energy.

So the Fourth Patriarch asked the Third Patriarch, "How do I achieve liberation?"

And the senior teacher said, "Who is it that is binding you?"

All the time experiences are coming up, yet often we say to ourselves that they are not good enough. Or the experience may be intense enough that we feel compelled to get rid of it. In body and being, we feel alienated and estranged, and we put ourselves in a bind. We can't tell how we really feel. Instead of really wanting to know about liberation, we want to know how we can have limitless energy and bodies and minds that don't experience anger or fear, because we don't want those around.

So then we ask the wrong question: "How can I get rid of this?" rather than "How can I receive this experience? How could I be thankful? What do I make of this?" Then there is no answer needed. Just be grateful. Just appreciate. This is why we say, "Practice being thankful." When you do this, there is no longer a need to act out as a way to eliminate the negativity that is inside. Easy does it.

One of the ways we practice being grateful is by bowing. From the outside this looks rather strange perhaps, but there is something about bringing your hands together and tilting your body that elicits gratitude. It's very mysterious. Already gratefulness is there.

Suzuki Roshi would say that bowing is receiving and respecting each thing as it is. Buddha bows to Buddha, and Buddha bows to himself. Even the heartache and the grief are something to bow to. And when we bow to them, we heal and become intimate with ourselves, and we become imperturbable, even though it may seem that we are quite upset.

In this sense, we don't have to be upset about being upset. So in some ways, gratitude is a doorway into our experience of the depth of our lives. It is also a doorway into connect-edness with others and the world. We stop holding out for more and holding out for better. Our hearts and beings soften, so we can receive the blessing inherent in the moment. Gratitude and thankfulness connect us with the world and with our own body and mind.

Don't Put Another Head
Above Your Own

Keep your head cool and your feet warm.
Don't put another head above your own.
Then, minute after minute, watch your step closely.
NYOGEN SENZAKI

What are the flavors that you enjoy? What are the foods that improve your vigor? Suzuki Roshi said that to find out for yourself in life is to own your own body and mind. Before he died, Nyogen Senzaki said, "Don't put another head on top of your own."[39] Our own heads are perfectly fine, especially when our heads are willing to listen to our bodies. Yet sometimes we become captivated and believe that another head knows better than ours.

When the head above our head is busy, it is already analyzing and assessing and telling us what to think, what

---

39 A Rinzai monk, Nyogen Senzaki was one of the earliest proponents of Zen in America, arriving in California in 1905. From the 1930s to 1950s, he established the "floating zendo" in the Los Angeles area. Senzaki transcribed the stories in Paul Reps's famous collection *Zen Flesh, Zen Bones: A Collection of Zen and Pre-Zen Writings* (Tokyo, Japan: Tuttle Publishing, 1957).

to do. Without this "head above our head" we can enter the depths of our lives. For example, if we eat an apple with the intention to be open to and receive the blessing and teaching of the apple, we taste it carefully. Then we know the apple deeply, and the heart of what we're experiencing touches our own hearts. This open, receptive practice is what makes things sacred.

This is why, in Zen, we say over and over again: *practice is realization; realization is practice.* When we practice receiving, being interested and attentive, then we have the realization that what is sacred is right here. We know it. We taste it. None of us can stay at this sacred place, but we can go back there. How? By tasting something carefully or listening carefully. We also access that place when we listen to our own bodies or our own beings, when we allow things to touch us.

When we experience things carefully, then we have a taste of realization. And in nurturing an open heart, that process continues endlessly.

Garnishes[40]

One thing I've observed is that garnishes often make the difference between an ordinary dish and one that is appetizing and flavorful. The garnish provides not only the final dash of color but also some elements of tart, pungent, earth and vibrant flavor. Moreover, the garnish shows that the cook is respecting and envisioning the food that is about to be served. How marvelous! If you do nothing but garnish every dish, your cooking will change overnight.

---

40   Adapted from *The Complete Tassajara Cookbook*, 29–30 and 243.

Fresh Green Herbs

Parsley, thyme, lemon thyme, marjoram, oregano, mint, basil, cilantro, tarragon, rosemary—these are the ones I use most. I include green onions or chives in this category as well. Aside from basil, cilantro, and tarragon, these grow in my garden most of the year, ready for use and waiting a few steps from the door.

Citrus Peel

Tartness is an important flavor component that often needs accentuating. Citrus peel—mostly lemon and orange—work well for this. I remove the colored part of the rind with a vegetable peeler and cut these into thin strips or mince as seems appropriate.

The Virtue of Radishes

The simplicity of this recipe is deceptive. Radishes in the supermarket often don't look too happy, and this dish depends on the goodness of the radishes, which probably has more to do with their upbringing than the creativity of the cook.

Radishes, round and red, white and elongated, or red with white—find radishes that delight you. You might have to go to a farmers' market or plant some in your yard or window box.

Wash the radishes, and remove the largest leaves. Arrange on a platter and serve with sweet butter and salt in little dishes on the side. This might be accompanied by sparkling juice or mildly alcoholic French sparkling cider.

IV

The Uncalled For

What to do amid calamity or confusion?
When my teacher first came to America,
he started cleaning his room.
I understand he cleaned for hours.
Cleaning establishes relationship.
Suzuki Roshi emphasized taking care
of all things right in front of you.

The Ten Thousand Idiots

It's important to remember that we've
all gotten to this point in our life honestly.
Most of us have simply been making our
best effort and this is where we are.

I've been practicing Buddhism now for more than forty years, and sometimes I don't know that I've gotten very far—on those days, for instance, when I'm yelling at things: sponges and dishes. I don't know if any of you ever do that sort of thing, but it feels embarrassing even if no one is watching.

A friend of mine said, "Well, that's refreshing because I never thought to yell at things. I always blame myself for my incompetence, and you blame the things for not behaving well enough."

It's still embarrassing.

The other day I came across a poem that was somewhat encouraging for me, and I'm going to share it with you, thinking that perhaps it will also be encouraging for you. It's a poem by Hafiz:

It is always a danger
To the aspirant
On the
Path

When one begins
To believe and
Act

As if the ten thousand idiots
Who so long ruled
And lived
Inside

Have all packed their bags
And skipped town
Or
Died.[41]

Apparently, I'm not in that grave a danger. Perhaps you aren't either, but maybe one or two of you are. Anyway, my ten thousand idiots are still around, and every so often, I call on them to entertain people.

I don't know about you, but I have very high standards for the kind of behavior that would be acceptable. That means that for much of my life my behavior has not been acceptable. I'm now in a movie you can see, and the unusual thing is that a movie was probably made about me because I am

41   Hafiz, "Ten Thousand Idiots," *The Subject Tonight Is Love: 60 Wild and Sweet Poems of Hafiz*, trans. Daniel Ladinsky (New York: Penguin Books, 1996), 51.

so less-than-well-behaved.[42] I thought practicing Buddhism meant you eventually attained good behavior, but it hasn't happened yet. I thought that eventually—well, maybe after forty years—I would be more impeccable.

When I mention this to people, they say, "Oh, you mean that you are human?"

And I think, *Oh yeah, I guess so.*

Is this a good thing, to be human? How do you feel about it? Allow me to be your therapist for a moment: How do you feel about this being-human business?

A lot of things happen for me in the kitchen. The other day, I went to put some leftovers into a small plastic container. I like to save leftovers—partly inspired by the Zen teaching that you should not waste even a single grain of rice: treat the food as though it were your eyesight. Is this such a problem? And what happens? The leftover container flips onto the floor. The soup is all over the floor. Do I deserve this? I'm doing spiritual practice here. I'm trying to treat the food really carefully. I'm trying to take care of these things, but what does the universe care? The container flips over.

I get angry at the things, and I'm being a good person. Is that good practice? Is it better to get angry at yourself or to be patient with yourself?

It's okay, little Eddie. You could have compassion for yourself.

A few minutes later, my most beautiful dish is sitting on the counter, and the next thing I know, it just slips off. Well, I might have barely grazed it with my robe or something. But it falls off. I thought maybe I could save it with my leg. Kicking

---

42   *How to Cook Your Life*, directed by Doris Dörrie (2007; Santa Monica, CA: Lionsgate, 2008), DVD.

at it, I did manage to hit it twice on its way down. I thought, with that kind of cushioning (because I had slowed it halfway down to the floor) it might land on the floor and be okay—but no. It's in twenty pieces, not a break that can be glued.

I have many glued things because I figure we've all been broken, and we're all put together. Life breaks us, and we put ourselves back together. Buddhism has the idea that Buddha puts us back together or Kwan Yin puts us back together. You don't necessarily need to do it yourself. Your body-mind heals itself—you have a new body. You have a fresh mind.

There is a story about Kannon, the bodhisattva of compassion (the Japanese use the names Kannon or Kanzeon, while the Chinese use the name Kwan Yin), who one day goes to hell to save all the beings there. In the Buddhist cosmology, hell is not endless. So Kannon goes there, intending to guide those in hell out of there. But the beings there are not very trusting.

They say, "Lady, we've heard this stuff before."

She says, "You could have this great life."

"Yeah, and credit card debt. What does it take?"

They don't believe her. It takes a lot of persuading. But finally, she gathers up all the people in hell and is leading them out, to another realm. Good going!

But then she looks back, and more people, great crowds of them, are wandering in, as though it's a fine place to hang out. They have no idea, not a clue, and she's devastated. She's worked so hard that now it blows her mind—literally, her head explodes.

At this time, Amida Buddha gives her another head. Kannon loses her head ten times before she has a head that can keep it together, so her statue has eleven heads, Eleven-Headed

Kannon. She has eleven heads because she endeavored to do impossible things with her good heart, her clear head. Finally, she has a head that can sustain this kind of impossible activity.

So maybe there's hope for me. Ten is just a number—like one thousand or one million. In Tibetan Buddhism, they have ten thousand prostrations and a hundred thousand offerings of various sorts. Maybe I have to break ten thousand bowls and spill a hundred thousand leftover containers of soup. Eventually, I will be able to keep it together when this happens. I don't know.

That same day, somehow I spilled the coffee, spilled the tea, spilled the water. It's all over the letters and the checks and the bills. Why are these things happening? And this isn't even something important, like health or friends with cancer or children or parents. These are just *things*. The ten thousand idiots are alive and well.

There are various pieces of advice in Zen. One I appreciate comes from the Zen teacher who said that because anger is so devastating and painful for both the person who is angry and those who are the objects of the anger, it is appropriate and important for the practitioner to "cut off all traces of anger." But since we're so—sorry to say—human, nobody can do this. "So," he says, "don't keep it in the forefront."

I remind myself of this piece of advice: don't keep it in the forefront. On the whole, our culture doesn't honor the inner world. It's hard in a culture that doesn't honor the inner world to honor your inner world. And if you're not honoring your inner world, what's becoming of your life? We end up going through the motions and making it look right or good. But what's going to be satisfying and fulfilling? How do we realize and express our good hearts?

From time to time, I realize that I'm in the right school. I'm a Zen teacher after all, who knows not to keep anger in the forefront. I am in the same school as Zen master Yakusan, who said, "Awkward in a hundred ways, clumsy in a thousand, still I go on."[43] I don't know what else to do—the ten thousand idiots remain alive and well.

---

43 Chinese Zen Master Yueh-Shan (Yakusan in Japanese).

Subtle Feeling Reveals Illumination

In a poem by Hafiz, he says, "Don't surrender your loneliness so quickly." You could also say your grief—don't surrender your grief so easily. We live in a culture that doesn't honor grief. People tell you to get over it. It can be your pet or your child or your parent or a friend who is sick or has died. People tell you, "Get over it. God has plans. You can have another child." If you're sad or grieving about something or lonely, there's not a lot of empathy for that. "Go for a walk. There's a dance on Friday night. There are terrific things you could be doing."

But Hafiz says, "Don't surrender your loneliness so quickly. Let it cut more deep."

This is what a meditation retreat will do. Your loneliness, your grief—it will cut more deep:

> Don't
> Surrender
> Your loneliness so quickly.
> Let it cut more
> Deep.

Let it ferment and season you
As few human
Or even divine ingredients can.

Something missing in my heart tonight
Has made my eyes so soft,
My voice so
Tender,

My need of God
Absolutely
Clear.[44]

In Buddhism, of course, it doesn't come from anywhere else. Each of us—our true nature—is the source. Our good heart surfaces when we sit with things, don't surrender them too easily—when we're willing to be with what's inside.

Here's another poem by William Stafford, who used to write a poem every day. It's called "For My Young Friends Who Are Afraid."

There is a country to cross you will
find in the corner of your eye, in
the quick slip of your foot—air far
down, a snap that might have caught.
And maybe for you, for me, a high, passing
voice that finds its way by being
afraid. That country is there, for us,
carried as it is crossed. What you fear

---

44 Hafiz, "My Eyes So Soft," *The Gift*, trans. Daniel Ladinsky (New York: Penguin Books, 1999), 277.

will not go away: it will take you into
yourself and bless you and keep you.
That's the world, and we all live there.[45]

To practice meditation is to practice great faith that you can enter into and settle in your inner world. You can live in your inner world and bring it to light in the outer world. It's not something you need to keep hidden until you think it's good enough. Otherwise, as some of my friends have said, you censor yourself before other people have the chance. When you are so careful, how can you say anything? To hazard speaking means we are engaging in the art or craft of being human. How do we do this? Can I sit and allow my inner world to be revealed, to be known, to be met, and to meet others?

In Zen, enlightenment is sometimes called intimacy. When you attain intimacy, it's not like you thought it would be. It's not what you expected. It's not some picture you dreamed up and then tried to make come true. Intimacy is what happens without your thinking about it.

There's a Zen story, or koan, in a collection known as *The Blue Cliff Record*. It's the story about the sixteen bodhisattvas who went to the baths. When they got in the water, they all attained realization and said, "Subtle feeling reveals illumination, and we are all children of the Buddha."[46]

Subtle feeling reveals illumination, and we are all children of the Buddha. For some of us, this is an important question:

---

45 William Stafford, "For My Young Friends Who Are Afraid," *Ask Me: 100 Essential Poems* (Minneapolis: Graywolf Press, 2014).

46 *The Blue Cliff Record,* trans. Thomas Cleary and J. C. Cleary (Boulder, CO: Shambhala, 2005).

Is it okay to be here in this world? Do you belong here? Do you have family here? There's nothing like being a child of the Buddha! Thich Nhat Hanh says we have blood ancestors and spiritual ancestors. It's helpful to have spiritual ancestors.

The sixteen bodhisattvas took a bath and said, "Subtle feeling reveals illumination, and we are all children of the Buddha." There is a commentary. You might be asking the same question as does the commentary: Lots of people get in the baths and get wet, but they don't attain realization. Why not? There are several answers.

In this particular koan, it says, "Because they stick to their skin and cling to their bones"—which is a little bit like me, the way I stick to "Why are these things out to get me? Why not go after the people who aren't cooking for themselves and give them challenges?"

Another answer to why "people get in the water, get wet, and don't attain realization" is that they are looking for a special experience. They are looking somewhere else. They say, "This can't be it," because it's not what they were looking for.

To stick to your skin and cling to your bones is to stay enmeshed in the horizontal world, where you dispense judgments and evaluations and initiate directives. When you open and receive the present moment, something more can come through—subtle feeling reveals illumination.

Here is another point from the commentary. Suppose your experience is not "subtle feeling that reveals illumination"? You have an experience and say to yourself, *This isn't subtle feeling reveals illumination. This is just another crummy event.* We do this all the time. You might be looking for some special experience that would make all the difference. But is it possible to let this moment be a moment with some blessing and compassion? A moment when the blessing and compassion of your good heart meet the pain and difficulty of your life? This, too, is subtle feeling revealing illumination, and "we are all children of the Buddha."

That's meditation. We sit. Sometimes something cracks open, and we sit in the midst of our good-heartedness, with our compassion and our love and our joy and our well-being, and it's pretty sweet.

Here's a little Buddhist prayer to end. This is a prayer the Dalai Lama uses from time to time. He suggests we recite it three times a day.

> With the wish to free all beings
> I shall always go for refuge
> to the Buddha, Dharma, and Sangha,
> until I reach full enlightenment.
>
> Enthused by wisdom and compassion
> Today in the Buddha's presence
> I generate the mind for full awakening
> For the benefit of all sentient beings.
>
> As long as space remains,
> As long as sentient beings remain,
> Until then, may I too remain
> And dispel the miseries of the world.[47]

---

47 His Holiness the Dalai Lama, *Practicing Wisdom: The Perfection of Shantideva's Bodhisattva Way* (Somerville, MA: Wisdom Publications, 2004), 165–166.

Sitting with Tragedy

Perhaps you've taken time to sit in silence with the sorrow of the tragedy in our lives here in America, with the school shootings in Connecticut.[48] I would like to take a little time now to sit quietly, holding this event inside in our hearts. It seems useful to sit right in the middle of things, so I'd like to take a few moments to do that.

There was a well-known Tibetan master, Marpa, who was the teacher of Milarepa, the great Tibetan saint. Marpa had an eight-year-old child who died, and he was grieving loudly. One of his students said, "But, Teacher, you always say that this is the world of illusion, so what are you crying about?" Marpa answered, "Yes, this is the world of illusion, and the death of a child is the cruelest illusion of them all, the most painful."

You've heard the First Noble Truth—life doesn't work the way we'd like it to. And we all have such pure, good, wonderful hearts—which, in Zen, we call true nature. We have a true nature that is undefiled, pure. But we can be estranged or disconnected from it, from our good hearts. Sometimes

---

48 On December 14, 2012, an emotionally disturbed young man murdered twenty-seven people, mostly first graders, at an elementary school in Newtown, Connecticut. The spree began at his home, where he killed his own mother. It ended when he shot and killed himself at the school.

we cannot find our way back to our good hearts, to our goodness, our kindness, our caring. We get very confused sometimes about what to do.

One of the most painful things is that not only do we get disconnected from our goodness, our love, our compassion, our good hearts, but it can also seem like people around us don't see it either. Sometimes we don't have support or others who see our blessedness. When others see our blessedness, it helps us to see it as well.

Another of the most touching qualities in our life, a characteristic of this good heart we have, is that we can take the pain and suffering of the world into our hearts and hold it there. Holding the pain or tragedy in our hearts, the harm or hurt that we see in ourselves and in others, we can come to some healing with it in our own world, in our own hearts.

This is different from trying to sort things out with your head. Your head asks, "Why did this happen?" But your heart doesn't need to know this. It can just breathe it in and hold it with some tenderness. Then you begin to realize that grief is out in the world and in here and that it's ongoing. It's been going on for as long as people have been here. Sitting with the tragedy, we discover—sometimes it takes awhile—that our hearts are strong and resilient. We carry on.

Sometimes we have a grief or tragedy or pain that breaks our hearts. In this case, the amazing thing is that a new heart comes in its place. It's even bigger and larger hearted. It can hold bigger pains and bigger tragedies. So, if you haven't already done so, I encourage you to bring pain, tragedy, hurt into your heart, into your good heart. Sometimes it will stir up your own grief. In some way, children are always our children. Children are our own inner child too—the child we were, who went through the pain we had. Any grief opens up all griefs.

A year after 9/11, I happened to be in London. I was at the Globe Theatre for a Shakespeare production on 9/11. Before the show, they wanted to take a minute to honor the victims of 9/11, but not just the victims of 9/11—also the victims of terrorism every day, everywhere it happens. It's happening every day.

So we sat quietly. That was interesting, to be in England. They didn't have quite the same view of the poor Americans, with our righteous indignation that we suffered from a terrorist attack. They wanted to acknowledge that all over the world people suffer from terrorism.

In sitting with this, a poem from Rumi came to me. It's about having a tender, soft place—each of us—in our hearts, that we might be able to remember, realize, abide in, express. It's a translation by Coleman Barks, who has given many years of his life, his heart, to putting Rumi's poetry into English, putting it into American free verse:

> Outside, the freezing desert night.
> This other night inside grows warm, kindling.
> Let the landscape be covered with thorny crust.
> We have a soft garden in here.
> The continents blasted,
> cities and little towns, everything
> become a scorched, blackened ball.
> The news we hear is full of grief for that future,

but the real news inside here
is there's no news at all.[49]

It is so important to grieve. Over the course of our lives, we rarely have opportunities to grieve. When we're small and our pets die, Mom and Dad are likely to say, "Don't cry. We'll get another one." Even if your child dies, people will say, "Oh, they're in a better place now." People have all kinds of explanations why not to grieve. So we have a chance for sorrow and to actually welcome the depths of human life into our hearts. Grief will bring you in touch with your heart and with all the sorrows of your life.

At the same time, it's also helpful to remember times in your life that were really sweet, really wonderful. Often it's a food experience. I remember my aunt's homemade bread. It was so good. Or the strawberries we picked down the road and the juice that ran down our faces. Or popsicles on a summer day. Frequently, we have memories of when we felt really happy and at home in this world.

Then, if you think about it, you may remember when you first realized that it doesn't work here. I remember when I was about seven, and I opened up the *San Francisco Chronicle* to check the baseball scores. It was 1952, and the front page said something about war in Korea. I said to my dad, "What is this word *war*?"

He said, "That's when people get guns, and they go out and shoot each other."

I said, "But why would they do that, Daddy? People could get killed!"

---

49   "The Tent," *The Essential Rumi*, 98–99.

He said, "I don't understand it either, but people have never figured out how not to have wars."

Little by little, we begin to realize that things don't always work out. You know people may say that when they were three or four years old, Mom and Dad were screaming at each other. They worried that one of them could be killed, and they didn't dare come out of their rooms. They hid. What was going to happen? Maybe this world isn't the safe place they thought it was, that they'd like to think it is.

We all have the capacity to stabilize ourselves and have our ground, to have our well-being and make our way in this world, not knowing what might happen. We can keep our awareness bright and awake, while seeing what's going on here, considering how we would like to respond, how we choose to respond.

It's important to work in the outer world and on your inner world. We can work on establishing our ground, finding our feet, finding our bodies, establishing our presence of mind, which is also, literally, presence of body. Then we look to see if we can find some way to connect our heart with the heart of the world, expressing our goodness and goodwill.

Rohatsu

Many years ago—it must have been about 1968—we were doing a sesshin with Suzuki Roshi. Traditionally, the eighth of December is Buddha's enlightenment day, and the seven days before that are often a meditation intensive: *Rohatsu Sesshin*. All over the world, the first week of December is a time for intense sesshin practice: sitting ten, twelve, fifteen periods a day, and sitting cross-legged for the three meals.

One of my students was at a recent sesshin in Berkeley. He said it never stopped being painful. Then he laughed. Zen people have a strange sense of humor, you know. "It didn't stop hurting. It never got any better."

I was reminded of the sesshin we did with Suzuki Roshi around 1968. One day, Suzuki Roshi said in his lecture, "The difficulties that you are now experiencing will continue," and he paused before finishing the thought, "for the rest of your life." We all laughed.

Right up until the end of his statement, we were all thinking that he was going to say something like, "The difficulties that you are now experiencing are just illusion. The difficulties you are now experiencing will continue until you have more compassion or enlightenment or awakening." How funny it was to think that we could arrive at a future without problems.

The nature of our lives shifts, yet when we actually pause and sit with ourselves, we can acknowledge how painful it is. We have less wishful thinking. All the thoughts beginning with "if only" lose much of their relevance.

And then my student said, "But I realized the one thing I could do was to care and to be tenderhearted with myself and to feel some tenderness and warmth toward my experience, toward the eating bowls, toward my pain, toward my difficulty. I could feel some warmth and tenderness."

This, of course, is basic Buddhist teaching. If there's an uneven, rocky road, do you want to cover the whole path with leather, or do you want to put the leather on your feet? What shall we do? Buddhism leans toward the side of "put the leather on your feet" rather than "let's fix the world."

People sometimes object to this approach, and I wouldn't eliminate either option. Why not see what you want to do? Maybe something will come to you that you want to do. What you want to do with the leather or the maker of the leather.

It's not obvious what might make a difference. Sometimes it's art or music or poetry or writing. Sometimes it's activity out in the world. What we can do is study and find our own way. We study carefully, to see what we can find out and to see what moves us inside, so that we may express ourselves in the world.

Lately, I've been remembering a Zen saying. I think the person who started using it might have been Zen Master Baso. He would say to his students, "Mind itself is Buddha." It helps here to remember that the word *mind* in Chinese and Japanese is *shin*, which is also the character for *heart*. It might be better for us to say, "Heart itself is Buddha," or we could say, "Awareness itself is Buddha." The word mind tends to be associated with intellect and conceptualization, and we might believe that it is separate from the body.

Sometimes, as it goes in Zen, somebody would approach Baso and say, "I hear you teach 'mind itself is Buddha.'"

Baso would say, "Not mind. Not Buddha." We use the word *buddha* here for something precious, something worthy, wise, compassionate, luminous, diamond-like, sparkling. Mind itself is Buddha. Mind is Buddha. Our awareness, our consciousness, is Buddha. Our heart is Buddha—something precious. Of course, we're in a world that says *this is precious and this isn't*. What is going to be precious, finally, in our culture, our world? As my student realized, "I could have a tender feeling for all these things."

One time Suzuki Roshi gave a talk about this saying, "Mind itself is Buddha," and he said, "Mind, consciousness, is Buddha. Itself, things are Buddha. Activity, action, movement, doing are also Buddha. Buddha of course is Buddha." Then, sure enough, he added, "And there is no Buddha." There's no fixed thing to designate as Buddha. In a sense, we could say Buddha is the capacity we have to find things precious, to find our life precious, to have grief, to have sorrow, to do our best to find our way in the world we live in.

Thank you for your effort and your good heart.

Zen Practice and Meeting
Early Childhood Trauma

Most of us have had some kind of trauma early in our lives. It's pretty much the way it is as human beings. We strive to create a persona that Mom and Dad will appreciate and like and that other people will appreciate and like as well. Perhaps the big people wanted us to quiet down or be more still. We really want to do this so that we are accepted in human society and in our families. We sense that we need to fit in so we will be cared for, so we don't get punished, so people like us, respect us, approve of us.

What do we need to do? This is the nature of life. Each of us has a story.

One of the wonderful things people notice about Zen practice is that when you sit in meditation and you face the wall, you soon realize you don't need to "do" that person anymore. Then you start to find you have problems. This is very interesting. You start to wonder, *Why am I practicing Zen? Am I doing this to have problems?* Within the community at Zen Center, people eventually drop the social face, the face they are used to "doing."

Thich Nhat Hanh teaches smiling practice. When you go for walking meditation, you practice enjoying yourself.

I asked him one time, "Why don't you teach mindfulness? Why do you teach enjoyment?"

He said, "You Westerners are enjoyment-challenged. Think about it, Ed. If you enjoy something, you have to be mindful of the object of awareness in order to enjoy it."

As we study, we begin to shift our focus. At the start we think, *How do I need to perform?* At some point, we get interested in, *How can I be me? How can I know myself and express myself instead of putting on a performance all the time?*

This is an ongoing study as far as I can tell. This is the study of a lifetime. We don't stop this study. We're also studying which situations call for what. I don't necessarily tell the clerk in the grocery store what I'm feeling when she asks, "How are you?" We're studying who we are with, what's the occasion, and who we share what with. If I tell the clerk that I'm actually feeling sad and anxious, the response may be, "Sorry I asked." So I may say, "Not bad."

How will you meet this occasion? How will you practice in this moment?

Robert Bly has something to say about all this:

One Source of Bad Information

There's a boy in you about three
Years old who hasn't learned a thing for thirty
Thousand years. Sometimes it's a girl.

This child had to make up its mind
How to save you from death. He said things like:
"Stay home. Avoid elevators. Eat only elk."

You live with this child, but you don't know it.
You're in the office, yes, but live with this boy
At night. He's uninformed, but he does want

To save your life. And he has. Because of this boy
You survived a lot. He's got six big ideas.
Five don't work. Right now he's repeating them to you.[50]

---

50   Robert Bly, *Eating the Honey of Words: New and Selected Poems* (New York: HarperCollins, 1999), 236.

Confronting War
and Uncertainty

In spite of all my practice in Buddhism, I am uncertain whether I am prepared to live in this world—it can be so painful. Last week I was mortified by the thought that we, as a country, might bomb innocent people—people who seem to have made the mistake of living in a country that has oil under the ground.[51] We might bomb people who somebody sees as disposable. Sometimes I think the world hasn't changed that much since the Middle Ages, since slavery. Wealth and power seem to covet wealth and power. They destroy anything in their way—including innocent people.

As Buddhists, we usually say we are not going to participate in that. But how do you participate in the world and fight for what you believe in and not become what you are fighting—become yourself evil? How do you do that? It's so easy to think that getting even will settle things, teach them a lesson. We understand how painful it is to be attacked by terrorists, but if we bomb Iraq, we judge the whole country, the entire population, to be sponsoring state terrorism. As Noam Chomsky points out, war is terrorism practiced by

---

51 On March 20, 2003, a coalition led by the United States invaded Iraq and began the long Iraq War.

those in power, and terrorism is war practiced by those not in power.

The problem is that it doesn't seem to work to crack down on terrorism. It just doesn't work. Look at what was done in Israel. Some reports say that after Israel cracked down on Palestinian terrorism, there were even more suicide bombings. But we keep thinking it will work because we have a righteous cause. It doesn't work. The more you crack down, the more the victims have real reason to hate you.

Buddhism is no different than other religions. We don't get to have a righteous cause. Regardless of religion or anything else, violence and hatred do not cease by violence and hatred. Violence and hatred only cease by love.

I was encouraged last week. I got an email from a friend who asked if anyone knows what we can do with our bodies to prevent this war. She got back an email suggesting she send half a cup of rice to the White House. It turns out you can send half a cup of uncooked rice to the White House for $1.06, and there is history to this.

In the fifties, there was a campaign by the Fellowship of Reconciliation to send rice to the White House to oppose a threatened war. Thousands of people sent rice to the White House, and it was never acknowledged. But ten years later, someone discovered that when President Eisenhower was dealing with Quemoy and Matsu, islands off the coast of China, and his advisors were telling him to bomb China, the president asked, "How many packets of rice did we get?" It had been tens of thousands.[52] He said, "If that many American people want to send rice to China, we can't bomb them."

---

52 First Taiwan Strait Crisis, 1954–1955, between the People's Republic of China and the Republic of China, backed by the United States.

I thought, *I'll send some rice with a little quote from the Bible, "If thine enemy is hungry, feed him."* In the package I included a note: "Please send this rice to the people of Iraq. Do not bomb them."

This is such a challenge for all of us. How do we fight evil without becoming evil? The Russian writer Aleksandr Solzhenitsyn said it well:

> If only it were all so simple! If only there were evil people somewhere insidiously committing evil deeds, and it were necessary only to separate them from the rest of us and destroy them. But the line dividing good and evil cuts through the heart of every human being. And who is willing to destroy a piece of his own heart?[53]

I don't know what to do. I don't know what to do about what will happen next. There is no way to tell. It doesn't seem to help to get lost in my own fear and terror. It doesn't help to believe we will live in safety. The next moment is fragile. It's vulnerable. It's free. It's liberated. It's empty, and it will appear.

One of the basic understandings in Buddhism is that we miss having the next moment when we add to it our evaluation: *It's good. It's bad. I like it. I don't like it.* When something unpleasant happens, we may think, *How can I ensure that moments like this never happen again?* It's just impossible. But it also seems impossible to give up trying to make the next moment come out one way instead of another. To allow the next moment simply to arise takes a great deal of courage.

---

53 Aleksandr Solzhenitsyn, *The Gulag Archipelago: 1918–56* (New York: Harvill Press, 2003).

Doing this, we develop a more subtle sense of how we participate in or cocreate each moment of our life. We respond more accurately to and with *things as it is* rather than to our story or our projections. This may include allowing our own response to things that arise and seeing if that response would be useful to act on or not.

One way to learn to do this is with meditation. In meditation, we see what happens next without controlling what happens and making it to our liking. This also means we are free.

If someone went to Suzuki Roshi during the Vietnam War and said, "Suzuki Roshi, there is a peace march on Saturday and I'm planning to go," he might say, "Good for you. Why don't you do that?" If someone said, "There's a peace march on Saturday, but I think I would rather sit meditation with you," he would say, "Oh, fine. Why don't you do that?" But when someone said, "How come we are meeting here when there is a war going on out there?" he became visibly angry. In a poignant episode recounted in David Chadwick's book *Crooked Cucumber,* he sprang to his feet and with his short Zen stick began hitting a student in the front room who had repeated the question, shouting, "You fools, you fools, you're wasting your time."[54]

After sitting down and catching his breath he said, "How can you expect to do anything in the world when you can't even tie your own shoes?"

My own feeling is that the sense of the question had been, "Shouldn't we all be out protesting?" and Roshi's response had been, "Don't you realize the war is right here?"

54 David Chadwick, *Crooked Cucumber: The Life and Zen Teaching of Shunryu Suzuki* (New York: Harmony, 2000), 318–319.

The war is right here, in each of our hearts. All of us are fighting the war in our hearts, and we are studying how to be friends to our own selves.

I find myself to be a pretty formidable foe: ornery, moody, intense, difficult to be with, and often gloomy, sad, or angry. What kind of person are you? We are finding out how we can be with ourselves and be happy being who we are. What will it take to be happy?

If we are only going to be happy under certain circumstances, then it won't happen very much. There are all these conditions: when I've had enough to eat, when I've been to the bathroom, when I don't want anything, when I am content, when the war is over, when everyone in the world is fed.

What are the criteria to be happy?

Buddha asked his disciples, "Does it make sense to make your happiness contingent upon conditions being met?" No, because then your happiness is always in the future, and the conditions are never finally met. If they are met, they are met for only a few moments, and then new conditions arise. We all know these conditions. They are endless: once I become a better person, once my lover forgives me, once people become nicer to me, once my parent does this or that. We put conditions on our happiness, which makes us the victims of our circumstances.

Buddhism says this is why we suffer. Is there some way to be happy regardless of conditions, to be happy without a cause? This is what we study in meditation. We study our thoughts and feelings and say "yes" to what comes up. *At last I am here, and I can be with myself and have some gratitude for my life, for my feelings and thoughts, for being alive in the world. I can be thankful.*

It turns out I can be someone who is happy, even with a lot of difficulties. I can breathe all my difficulties into my heart or breathe in all the difficulties of another person. I can sit quietly with someone who is having difficulty, which begins once I stop telling myself things like, *What's wrong with you, you idiot? You shouldn't have any difficulties now. You've been a Buddhist for so long.*

Mark Twain said, "I've lived through some terrible things in my life, some of which actually happened."[55] That seems like a good happiness to aim for: happiness without any conditions that need to be met. We are here, and we can sit quietly in our lives and nurture happiness beyond conditions.

If you are moved to do something, whether it's sending rice to the White House or whatever, please be moved. A fundamental point for each of us is what will we do with our lives?

Mother Teresa said she started her spiritual practice by helping one person. We all start some place, and that is an expression of our life. Part of it we have no control over, but some of it we do. For that, we have the capacity to find ways to express our gifts, to give to the world in the best way we know how. We make our effort each moment.

---

55 *Washington Post*, September 11, 1910; *Reader's Digest*, April 1934.

The Secret to Life

I'm finally ready to tell you the secret of life. Of course, it's not really a secret. It's just that we hide this piece of information from ourselves and go on as though it were a secret. The secret to life is enjoyment.

Some of you might get this right away. *Of course. Enjoyment.* But most of you will ask, "Enjoyment?" The concept is a bit scary. When I mention to people, "Please enjoy your food," they may say, "If I enjoyed my food, I'd be a blimp." So let's examine what enjoyment is and what it isn't. When does enjoyment turn into lust and greed? If you've become a blimp by enjoyment, then your devotion to enjoyment has not been serious enough. Your practice of enjoyment has slipped.

We also have the notion that if we had enjoyment we would fall in love rather easily and have unwanted pregnancies and all kinds of catastrophes. I feel like I have to talk about this to reassure you that the practice of enjoyment could actually benefit you and allow you to go forward.

Zen Master Dōgen says that enjoyment is one of the dharma gates. Enjoyment is also one of the five factors of concentrative absorption, or samadhi. The initial stage of absorption includes enjoyment. It's also one of the thirty-seven wings of enlightenment, and in another list it is one of the seven factors or limbs of enlightenment. (So I'm not just making this up.)

Enjoyment is when we have a feeling of connecting with the object of our awareness, and we allow it to move us. Your awareness, or consciousness, resonates with the object of awareness—resonates, vibrates, hums with, attunes to. In aikido they call it "blending with." You blend your energy. When your consciousness connects with the object of awareness and resonates, vibrates, hums, and blends, you are moved by and can move the object of awareness. You are that connected.

There's enjoyment that is naturally enjoyment—something happens and you enjoy it—and then there are times when you can cultivate enjoyment. Knowing that we can cultivate enjoyment is important, because one of the ways Buddhism says we suffer is that we think our enjoyment depends on the object of consciousness. When we believe that enjoyment depends on the object, then we feel we need to control our surroundings in order to experience joy. We have to get the right object, the one that is going to elicit the enjoyment in us. If I have the chocolate cake, I could have enjoyment until I'm too full to have enjoyment from the chocolate cake. Then I would have more enjoyment from not eating the chocolate cake than I would have from continuing to eat the cake. When you observe your experience, your level of enjoyment, carefully, you make wiser decisions.

This is practice. This is "subtle feeling reveals illumination." We think, *I need this object.* We think, *If somebody smiles at me, I could have enjoyment. If somebody frowns or is angry or upset or scared or sad or disappointed, I won't have enjoyment. I need them not to do those things, and I need them to do the other things that give me enjoyment. If others would behave the way I want them to behave, then I could have my enjoyment. So would you stop that?*

Because we believe our enjoyment is dependent on the object, we try to control the object. *Shut up. Go over there. Come over here.* We try to get the things that would be enjoyable to be here, and to get the things that wouldn't be enjoyable over there, somewhere else. How well does this work? Buddhism teaches, "It doesn't work very well, now does it?"

The things you don't enjoy often show up right in your face. The things you enjoy are somehow over there. It's exactly the opposite of what you were thinking. And you keep thinking that if you just had a better way to control all these things—but that doesn't work either. It's very frustrating to become a Buddhist and still have the idea of controlling and manipulating objects—people, things, the weather, your body, your breath, sensations, thoughts, feelings. Trying to control these objects of awareness is called suffering, because it cannot be done.

Instead, you could practice enjoying whatever happens to show up. Is that simple or what? *But how do you enjoy pain? How do you enjoy sickness? How do you enjoy fatigue? How do you enjoy anger? These things are not enjoyable. You're telling me to enjoy them? That's crazy.*

But the concept of enjoyment in Buddhism is that your awareness could actually connect with the object, whether it is work or play, a joy or a sorrow. Your consciousness could receive and connect with that object and resonate, even with frustration, sadness, disappointment, fatigue—and certainly with energy, joy, and delight. This is also called compassion. Sometimes it is called acceptance. It could be called forgiveness. It could be called gratitude. Here we are calling it enjoyment.

This is different from our usual idea of how to have happiness. Our usual idea is to touch the things we are comfortable touching and not to have to touch or be touched by those other things that are so disgusting. Consequently, we spend a good deal of our lives being out of touch—literally out of touch—with sensations, with feelings, with thoughts, with people in our lives, with the world around us. As soon as we are touched, one of those bad things might happen—one of those things that is unpleasant or painful or disgusting. So our default habit may be "not-touching."

For many years now, Thich Nhat Hanh has taught, "Please enjoy your breath." When we had a retreat with him at Green Gulch Farm in the early eighties, he told us that to practice enjoyment we needed to focus, pay attention, concentrate, give our awareness to the object. You attune your awareness with the object of awareness—in this case, your breath. You allow your breath to in-form you (as it pleases) rather than telling your breath how to breathe better—that is, in a way that would be more preferable to you. You allow your body to be moved by your breath. There arises a level of enjoyment that is pure sensation. You are allowing the sensations of your breathing, of your being, to arise and disappear with enjoyment, resonating.

When you're interested in connection and connecting with yourself, your own being, with another, with the world, with realization, then you allow yourself to be touched by sensation and to touch with your awareness. William Blake had this idea centuries ago: "the whole of creation will be consumed and appear infinite and holy, whereas it now appears finite and corrupt. This will come to pass by an improvement of sensual enjoyment."[56]

The world appearing infinite and holy "will come to pass by an improvement of sensual enjoyment" that you can sense with your being. "But first the notion that man has a body distinct from his soul is to be expunged," according to Blake. The notion that body and consciousness are separate—you would have to let go of that.

Then Blake said, "If the doors of perception were cleansed everything would appear to man as it is, infinite." This is enjoyment. Mostly our doors of perception are not very clean, and we have the idea that the body and mind are separate. We also have the idea that the mind is strong and the body is weak. Actually, it's the other way around: The body is strong. The mind is the weak one. Though neither arises without the other, we often fail to realize how faithful the body is and how willing. We like to think that the mind is in charge, but who knows better how to breathe, you (the mind) or the breath (the body)?

Hands love to do stuff. They love to work hard and get in the dirt and play and do things, to pick up guitars and strum. Hands love to scrub things, knead bread, caress cheeks. Meanwhile, the mind may say, "I don't feel like it. Not today. It's too hot." It's often the mind that becomes reluctant. Then the hands may be saying, "Good grief! Is this depressing or what? I don't get to do anything. That fellow up there doesn't feel like it today." Hands like to be touched and to touch. It doesn't matter what it is. It can be sponges, pots, pans, floors,

---

56 William Blake, "The Marriage of Heaven and Hell," *The Portable Blake*, ed. Alfred Kazin (New York: Penguin Classics, 1977), 249.

brooms, cups, pianos, guitars, faces, laundry, the air. Hands love being hands and touching, fiddling, working.

In the summer of 1967, Brother David Steindl-Rast, the Benedictine monk, came to Tassajara for the very first practice period. I was the head cook. Brother David was the head dishwasher. So I would thank Brother David often. He was a true bodhisattva. No matter how hard he worked, people just kept bringing him more dirty dishes. It was never done. He cleaned things, and people brought them back dirty. They didn't say, "Thank you for cleaning it. Now we'll take care of it. We'll venerate it. We'll honor it. We'll put it on the altar." No. They simply kept making things dirty again. So I would thank Brother David, the great bodhisattva of Tassajara.

Brother David once said that everything in life is a gift from God. This is a Christian way of putting it. But for it to be a gift from God, you have to receive it as though it were a gift from God. If you say, "No, I don't want this gift. I don't see this experience as a gift," that's called sin. Sin is when you do not sense that this moment is a gift from God and you don't want to appreciate it. That's called sin. And according to Brother David, they tried to get rid of that heresy of the division of mind and body back in the third or fourth century.

So your desire is a gift from God. When we get desire in life—wanting to eat or to have a relationship—often the first thing we want to do is get rid of it. Where is the gift of the desire and connecting with the desire and being moved by having desire?

Enjoyment is not an easy practice, but it's where connection is. It's where intimacy is. It's where our real vitality and our real joy and our energy reside.

Enjoyment, Excitement, Greed, and Lust

I want to talk about the differences between enjoyment, excitement, greed, and lust because it's easy to confuse these. Why don't I talk about this in terms of food, since it's a subject I've spent a fair amount of time studying? I've spent a fair amount of time studying any number of things, but food seems a good place to start tonight.

We do the ceremony of eating food in our Zen practice periods, and during this meal ceremony, we serve each other food. Serving each other food in silence turns out to be one of the most intimate things we can do with another person. It's that intense. The server and the receiver first bow to each other. Then the servers put the pot of food down, and the person eating picks up their bowl to be served. You are so present with each other. In the silence, you sense people's anxiety, fear, desire, greed, lust, disappointment, confusion, anger, hurt, perhaps their calm and buoyancy. Right away, in this simple exchange, you meet somebody.

When you eat in silence, you notice more carefully what you're doing. Greed is when you have food in your mouth that is so delicious you need to get rid of it so you can get more. You need to not experience the food you have in your mouth so you can get rid of the food in your bowl and get seconds. That's not enjoyment. That's eating faster and getting through the experience so you can get more of this wonderful thing that you are not actually having.

This is excitement, and when it is more intense, we call it greed or lust. You're chasing something, though you are not experiencing what you have. You need to get rid of what you have so you can get on to the experience that you could have, though it's likely you won't have the new experience either because you're busy chasing after the next moment. This can be extremely intense. You can be enthralled and caught up in it, but it's not enjoyment. And you are not connecting with the food. You're not tasting much of anything. The excitement is taking all your attention.

I did this for a while. I used to eat two bowls of cereal, two bowls of nuts, two bowls of fruit, two bowls of everything. I had to eat very fast because we don't have that much time when we're in the meditation hall. Then I thought, *Why don't I just taste the food?* This is enjoyment, to actually taste what's in your mouth, to have it and appreciate it and connect with it and be touched and savor it. I began eating a third as much, and I wasn't hungry. Before, I was always hungry.

Sometimes it felt as though we were having contests to see who could eat the most. We had yeasted bread and unyeasted bread, and we had peanut butter or butter or jam to put on the bread. We would eat twelve, fourteen, sixteen, eighteen half slices of bread for lunch. It was a frenzy. But there was no enjoyment of actually savoring and being present with and receiving and being moved and touched and nourished. You can't be nourished when you're greedy about taking in, not actually experiencing what you take in.

You have a sense of being a hungry ghost. No matter how much you take in, you're still hungry because you never get nourished. You never have the sensation of touching, tasting, swallowing.

This is excitement. You start eating, and it gets so exciting that you no longer have the food to savor or taste. The food is fuel to perpetuate the excitement. Instead of connecting with or having some meeting or touching and being touched by food, you use the food to have your excitement. Again, you don't end up having nourishment or sustenance or well-being because you feel used.

Sometimes we say to our bodies, "Give me something better. What you're doing is not good enough. It's not exciting enough. It's not pleasurable enough. Can't you do better than that? Why haven't you enlightened me yet? Get it together. Shape up." We ask our bodies to produce some better experience for us. Then our bodies, our beings, feel used.

When you are willing to touch and be touched by your experience, by the sensations that are arising, that turns out to be nourishing. Our awareness is cleansed of greed and lust, excitement and other tendencies that otherwise whip us about. Then when we meet something, we have a sense of vastness, of the infinite. We call that joy.

This joy is not dependent on any particular object. It's not dependent on you controlling things, not having anger, not having sadness. These are all gifts that you could receive and be with and appreciate—gifts you could enjoy. This elicits *sukha*, or ease, because you don't have to manipulate and control and chase after something to enjoy. It's already here. It's your own capacity to connect and be with and receive the gifts of each moment.

Please enjoy your breath, the heat, the cold, whatever happens to come. See what you can do about being with your life each moment.

When Is Adversity Useful?

When is adversity useful to us, or at least instructive? There was a wonderful story recently in *The New Yorker* about a Zen monk in Japan, where there is something of a cult of suicide.[57] He was working with people who were suicidal, and he was emailing them and calling them and trying to help them.

The article told about his background; he was in one of the really rigorous Rinzai Zen schools, where they do intense difficult practice. They got up really early, did zazen for long, long hours, and also worked. The monk did this for three or four years. It was a place where there were not many other monks, and it was so difficult that most of the sensible ones had left.

Finally, they were going to have the big sesshin of the year, the Rohatsu sesshin, which takes place in December. At this monk's temple during Rohatsu, no one sleeps for a week. They meditate day and night. The monk was going to be the cook for this sesshin, so for the week before, he didn't sleep either.

---

57   The monk is Ittetsu Nemoto. See Larissa MacFarquhar, "Last Call," *The New Yorker*, June 24, 2013.

About the third day of sesshin, this monk was moving a giant pot of soup and was totally at the end of his resources. He thought, *I can't do this. I'm going to drop it. I think I am dying.* At that moment, a huge wave of energy came over him. Whew! He was filled with a vast energy, as if he had been reborn and knew he could do anything.

Soon after that, after realizing he could do anything, the monk decided to leave the monastery. With no plan, he realized he would be fine.

So he took off his robes, put on street clothes, and went to Tokyo. He got a job flipping burgers. The owners soon found him to be an unusual employee. Flipping burgers, he was always so happy. The owners would say, "Hey, are you okay? You've been working a long time."

"Oh, yes. I am just fine. Really great here. Loving it."

"But aren't you hot? It's really hot back there."

"Oh, yes. It is really hot. But it's just fine. Don't worry. Not a problem."

Then business started picking up. Everyone wanted this happy burger flipper to make their burger. And they wanted to talk to him: "Okay, what is your secret?" So he started talking to people and using this happy energy that seemed to be pouring through him. People wanted to talk to the happy burger flipper about their problems.

Eventually, he left the burger place and decided to devote himself full time to helping people who were suicidal. He put on his robes again and moved to his own little temple way out in the countryside.

Japan has the highest rate of suicide in the world; there is a whole culture around it. In talking to many depressed and suicidal people, the monk found it was difficult, even for a happy monk. There was a cost. Soon he had heart problems and blood pressure issues. He wasn't sure he was helping. He realized that too many of his conversations were online, and he wanted to meet these people if he was going to try to help them.

It turns out there are hundreds of thousands of people in Japan—many of them young people—who stay on the internet in their rooms and never leave. They're called *Hikikomori*—"social shut-ins." Many of the parents of these young people bring them food. The monk said, "In the future, if I am going to try to help you, you'll have to come and meet me face-to-face."

This worked a lot better. In one case, a troubled kid who was on the verge of suicide made the effort to go and see him, which required a train ride and a five-hour walk. When he arrived, he told the monk, "Excuse me, but I don't need to talk to you. On the way here, I was walking for hours, and I figured everything out."

So it is for us with our adversity. Get out of the house occasionally. Go walking. Do a little gardening. Let the energy move through you and see what will be expressed.

Bugs in a Bowl

Why do we meditate? My teacher said lots of things
about that, but one in particular has stuck with me:
"We do this practice to purify our love."

When I look at the people at Tassajara, I see so much blessedness. On one hand, there's not a lot to tell you. Here we are
in the midst of enlightenment unfolding—and yet there's
still some problems. It's not quite as good as it could be, is it?
Darn! People may point to various things as the problem, yet
one way or another, some likes and dislikes creep in around
the edges, along with judgments of good and bad and right
and wrong. Still and all, reality goes on unfolding beyond
our capacities to reform it.

We argue with the way things are. We're disappointed that
reality is not quite the way we set out to make it, according
to the picture we had in mind. So now what? I want to talk
a bit about how things are, and, of course, there are different
ways of talking about this, so I have a poem for you. I've
been enjoying this poem a lot lately. It's a poem by Antonio
Machado, more or less the version by Robert Bly.

Last night, as I was sleeping,
I dreamt—marvelous error!—
that a spring was breaking
out in my heart.
I said: Along which secret aqueduct,
Oh water, are you coming to me,
water of a new life
that I have never drunk?

Last night, as I was sleeping,
I dreamt—marvelous error!—
that I had a beehive
here inside my heart.
And the golden bees
were making white combs
and sweet honey
from my old failures.

Last night, as I was sleeping,
I dreamt—marvelous error!—
that a fiery sun was giving
light inside my heart.
It was fiery because I felt
warmth as from a hearth,
and sun because it gave light
and brought tears to my eyes.

Last night, as I slept,
I dreamt—marvelous error!—
That it was God I had
here inside my heart.[58]

---

58 Antonio Machado, "Last Night As I Was Sleeping," trans. Robert Bly, in
    Times Alone: Selected Poems of Antonio Machado (Middletown, CT: Wesleyan,
    1983), 43.

So often, if reality is not the way we want it to be—if we have difficulty with someone or if we're tired or stressed—we try to figure out what to do about it, and it's very tempting, when your strategies aren't working, to do them harder and more devotedly. We believe that if we do them thoroughly enough, they're going to work finally. But will they really? We believe that with our persistent efforts reality will come around, and those other people will agree to behave in the way, finally, that we've always wanted them to because we're judging them so severely that they're going to want us to stop judging them like that. Of course, this cannot be done! And at some point, we may notice that the others are shaking their heads at our futile efforts.

So instead of this, you see, Antonio Machado had a dream. A spring is breaking out. There's some refreshment here inside the heart—"water of a new life / that I have never drunk." There is a beehive. The heart is full of activity, turning pollen into honey out of, he says, "my old failures." That's pretty sweet.

So we're in this funny business called Zen because there's no way to get it right and make things happen the way they're supposed to. And it's surprisingly faith-based or trust-based. Dōgen, for instance, says you should realize that the true dharma emerges of itself, clearing away hindrances and obstacles. You should know the true dharma emerges of itself, and in this case, we could say like a spring in your heart or a beehive or a fiery sun that brings tears to your eyes.

Suzuki Roshi said, "You want truth. You want beauty or righteousness or virtue, and you set out to attain it. But it isn't always so. I have nothing like that for you . . . When you realize you can't attain that, then your way of looking and speaking will be different. The way of life you choose will be different."

You won't be setting out to manufacture reality according to your picture of the way it should be. And you might play or live more creatively with the way things are.

What is the nature of reality? Nothing is fixed, yet we tell ourselves a story. We hear something, we believe something about reality, and then we start behaving that way, being afraid because something happened to us, years ago, when we were betrayed or hurt in some way. Maybe we're wishing and longing for something, and we're waiting. What shall we do in the meantime? How do we act? The nature of mind seems to be that there's no way to figure this out, to get it right.

There's more to be said for the fact that we have a kind of vision. We have an imagination. We've had various experiences in our lives that are like a vision or a flash or an insight, and then we work on how to live out our heart's desire, the truth of our vows in the bones and marrow of our life. How do we do that? How do we bring forth what's precious from inside? Where is the place to do that, and who do we do that with?

This is different from studying skills and developing techniques and strategies and plans. It comes out of our being. It's an act of creation—we create our life. We create our reality. We could create it with this kind of openness about reality. It's not one way or another. There are not necessarily any threats out there. Or maybe there are. Or maybe there aren't.

I have another poem I want to share. It's called "Bugs in a Bowl." It's by David Budbill, who lived up in the mountains, writing poems. He says:

Han Shan, that great and crazy, wonder-filled
Chinese poet of a thousand years ago, said:

*We're just like bugs in a bowl. All day
going around never leaving their bowl.*

I say, That's right! Every day climbing up
the steep sides, sliding back.

Over and over again. Around and around.
Up and back down.

Sit in the bottom of the bowl, head in your hands,
cry, moan, feel sorry for yourself.

Or. Look around. See your fellow bugs.
Walk around.

Say, Hey, how you doin'?
Say, Nice bowl![59]

Sometimes it seems like kind of a no-brainer, doesn't it, to let go of your picture of reality and the way reality could be, and to go ahead and interact, play, meet, engage, endeavor, work? Maybe even do a little Zen and yoga. Explore your good-heartedness. See your fellow bugs.

---

59   David Budbill, "Bugs in a Bowl," *Moment to Moment: Poems of a Mountain Recluse* (Port Townsend, WA: Copper Canyon Press, 1999), 53.

V

Bites

Don't just do what you're told.
Find your experience.
If you're eating, taste what you put in your mouth.
What a concept—to taste what you're eating!

Is My Practice Working?

In the late sixties, when the back-to-the-land, turn-on, tune-in, drop-out counterculture was in full swing, the People's Baker baked bread and gave it away for free. But was that true freedom?

Once, Suzuki Roshi told us in a lecture: "Your culture is based on ideas of self-improvement. Improvement means that instead of going to Japan by ship, now you can go by jumbo jet." So improvement is based on comparative value, which is also the basis of our society and our economy.

"I understand that you are rejecting that idea of (material) civilization, but you are not rejecting the idea of improvement. You still try to improve something. Isn't that rather materialistic? Buddhists do not hold so strongly to the idea of improvement."

Some months later, when I tried to use that as an excuse not to practice hard, Roshi said, "Ed, if your practice is not advancing, it's going downhill backwards fast."

So what is this "advancing" that is not getting caught up in improvement? And wouldn't the real way to improve be everyday mind as the way?

At a later sesshin, Roshi talked about what is ordinary and what is special.

"What is ordinary," he said, "is to strive after something you think is special. What is truly special is to abide in the ordinary. You are here. Always here.

Even though you say your practice is not good enough, there is no other practice for you right now. Good or bad, it is your practice. To approach perfect practice, there is no way other than to accept yourself. To say your practice is bad does not help your practice. To say your practice is excellent does not help. Your practice is your practice."

To assess if my practice is working means looking at my idea of what I thought practice would or would not do (and who is saying so). I asked Darlene, my dharma friend of more than thirty years, if her practice is working. Her "I don't think so" is cheerful, bright, and buoyant. "Because," she explains without further prompting, "I have the idea that if my practice were working, things would go along much more smoothly than they do. But maybe that's the wrong idea. If 'my practice working' means that I am having lots of intimate encounters with other people where I might get slapped down, knocked down, or put down—well, then my practice is spectacular."

What, after all, would liberation look like? How would you know if *this* was enlightenment? Do you have eyes to see? Your practice is your practice.

Beginner's Mind

One of Suzuki Roshi's favorite and most-quoted expressions is "beginner's mind." To practice Zen is to practice having beginner's mind. "In the beginner's mind there are many possibilities, but in the expert's there are few."[60] He said that even if you do Zen practice for many years, it's important to maintain or renew your beginner's mind, seeing what you can find out, studying, being open.

Roshi also said that "Zen is to feel your way along in the dark." You don't know where you are going or what you will find. You might think it's better to know where you are going and how to get there so that you can just do it. But when you know where to go and how to get there, you push people and things out of your way. *Out of my way! I know where I'm going.* Then you are not so sensitive. You are in a hurry.

In Zen, it's better not to know where you are going or what you will find, Roshi told us. Then you are careful. You're sensitive. *What is this? What is it I am meeting? What is this moment? How shall I live my life?*

---

60 Shunryu Suzuki, "Prologue," *Zen Mind, Beginner's Mind: Informal Talks on Zen Meditation and Practice* (Boston: Shambhala, 2006), 1.

So it's pretty nice to walk into a whole roomful of people lost in the dark. Thank you for being here. In this darkness, we can be friends and not be in too much of a hurry to get anywhere.

Suzuki Roshi brought up another topic from time to time, how in meditation you often notice something you hadn't noticed before. One day he was working in the garden moving rocks and didn't realize how tired his muscles were until he started sitting.

"When I started sitting, I thought, *Oh, my muscles are in pretty bad condition*. You might think it would be easier to practice meditation and live your life if you didn't have problems. But when you practice right there in the midst of your difficulty, finding your way with your difficulty, then you are open to possibilities, and you find your way. It's not such a good idea to spend your life hiding your problems."

What Was Said to the Rose

Here is a line from a poem by Rumi that has to do with what happens to us in our lives as we grow up and mature and age: "What was said to the rose that made it bloom is being spoken here in my heart now."[61] Suzuki Roshi called this "sincere practice." He said, "Listen carefully to your inner voice. It is the voice of your heart." As you listen carefully to your inner voice, you will find what was spoken to the rose that made it bloom. And it will help you bloom.

Katagiri Roshi said, "Let the flower of your life force bloom." Let your life take shape and form to help you appear in the world, to help bring what is inside out into the world. Express yourself—listen and receive and express.

Dōgen Zenji said, "Let things come and abide in your heart. Let your heart respond. Let your heart go out and abide in things." Relate to the things of the world. Study how to let them into your life and connect with them. Respond to them. Instead of having an idea what your life should look like or what the results should be, give your attention to things and let things come to you. Let the response come from your heart.

---

61   Rumi, "What Was Said to the Rose," *A Year with Rumi: Daily Readings*, trans. Coleman Barks (New York: HarperCollins, 2006), 147.

Bewildered?

Sometimes we are bewildered, and it is useful to recognize that. We always start from where we are. So we start in bewilderment, concerned that we may take inappropriate action until we develop clarity.

But then we can study. *What have I been bumping into?* See what is coming up with the confusion.

And maybe we can be careful not to blame, as we feel more love and connection with the process, as it unfolds. Blame blinds us.

In the meantime, here's the big news: who you think you are is a trance, an idea.

We have lots of comments: "I am not perfect." "I am unhappy." "I am lonely and hopeless." "I must somehow fix what is wrong with me." It's a trance you can dispel.

Life itself is the same stuff—the same consciousness. The waves are not separate from the ocean. Thus, if you have flaws, then flaws must be everywhere. Which means that virtue or goodness must be everywhere. And "who you are" cannot be held as a concept. It can't be held at all. You can only be experienced, and when you really experience things closely, often they become quite funny. Humor is a sign of becoming disconnected from the trance of who you think you are.

Indeed, instead of buying into "poor me," you can focus on the quality of the inner dialogue. Amazing material, isn't it? But at times so repetitive! Keep looking inside. Eventually, something will change. Clarity might arise, or at least the patience to continue with not knowing exactly. You could ask the voices inside to come up with new stories.

"The treasure house within you will open, and you are free to use it as you wish," said Zen Master Dōgen. You don't need to seek outside.

No Masterpieces,
Just Cooking

At the suggestion of others, I decided to make some Zen-and-cooking videos and immediately ran into problems. My idea was that there would be cooking instructions and a little Zen teaching and perhaps some stories. I wanted to do a cooking show that is different from most others. Not just recipes; not just the usual.

In a little blurb written up to promote the show, someone wrote, "And Ed will teach inveterate meat eaters how to create vegetarian masterpieces." I was unhappy. Excuse me, but what is this preoccupation with masterpieces? We aren't supposed to cook unless we can make a masterpiece? We aren't supposed to live our lives unless they can be brilliant?

Well, no wonder so few of us are in the kitchen. We go out to eat because we say, "Oh, I can't make a masterpiece." I just want to encourage people to cook! Without focusing on masterpieces, could we please go ahead and simply cook something moderately good? And have a good time and enjoy eating it? And have some friends over and enjoy each other's company?

Let's be real. As much as anything, I want to encourage this kind of offering in the kitchen. This is generosity of spirit.

You cook something and you offer it. That's enough and ultimately satisfying and nourishing. And you encourage others to inhabit the kitchen and do likewise.

Meal Chant

We venerate the three treasures
and give thanks for this food,
the work of many people,
the offering of other forms of life.
May this food nourish us,
body, mind, and spirit.
May all beings be happy,
healthy, and free from suffering.
Blessings.

Soft Mind

Suzuki Roshi, from time to time, would talk about soft mind. He said to practice Zen is to have soft mind. Soft mind is not to be in any particular hurry to get anywhere or to obtain a particular experience that we think would be better than the current one.

If we try to get something better, we notice our minds getting hard and often our bodies too. Bottom-line thinking emphasizes being hardheaded rather than soft-minded. Of course that hardness can translate into fragility. We could break or come apart—maybe even shatter. What a mess!

So in Zen practice we may come apart. Sometimes people say when they are sitting, "This zazen is driving me crazy. I can't stand it, sitting here on this zafu." We could call that "getting softened up"—rather than enlisting a hard mind to ensure that we get our way, our mind becomes soft enough and flexible enough to be with things.

We have resources in our lives. Sometimes, if we are hard-minded, we feel as though we have none or they're not good enough. But when we are soft-minded, the resources are right at hand. We can feel around in the dark for them.

Dōgen says our treasure house will open of itself, and we will spend freely. The power of our lives and the vitality and health of being a human being reveal themselves to us.

We taste what is in our mouths, see what is before our eyes, and allow things to touch the center of our being. The sacred is there, gratitude is there, and all our resources manifest in bounty.

```
GETTING STARTED

Washing my hands, preparing to handle food,
I cleanse my mind of same old thinking,
and offer to lend a hand,
freshly doing each task.
```

Misfits

Life is up to you. Though you cannot figure it out,
you can feel your way along. Nobody else can take over
your position. Nobody else can be you. Study carefully.
You can find your own vitality, your own gifts...

I think this is an amazing practice that we do and life that we live together, though it's hard sometimes to see the benefits. But I'm like many others. Practicing Zen, I think, saved my life.

Phillip Wilson was one of Suzuki Roshi's students many years ago. Phillip loved Roshi. You see pictures of him helping Roshi move rocks. Phillip also loved to party, but he knew that if he went home after a party, he would never get to zazen the next day. So he would drive his car over to Laguna Street outside the Zen Center, park his car, and go to sleep. Then he could get up in the morning and go in to zazen. "I didn't want to miss zazen," he said, "and I didn't want to miss the party."

Phillip was a large, muscular man. He had been a football player on the Stanford offensive line. One year he decided that nothing would get in his way. Nothing would stop him. Often by the third quarter of games, he said he would be performing on the field while his awareness was watching the action from above the field. He would exhaust himself so completely that afterward the team doctors would take him to the hospital and have him put on IV fluids while he came down from his high and recovered his energy and stamina.

Phillip studied Zen in Japan; Suzuki Roshi sent him to Eihei-ji Monastery, even though he didn't know any Japanese. At Tassajara, he lived in cabin 14. Once, when Roshi went to San Francisco, Phillip stopped following the schedule. He had a battery-powered 45-rpm record player, and we could hear Iron Butterfly and Chubby Checker's "Let's Do the Twist" all over Tassajara Valley.

When Suzuki Roshi came back, we saw Phillip going to visit Roshi in his cabin. Then we heard Roshi hitting him. *Whack! Whack! Whack!*

We all thought Roshi was hitting him for playing a 45-rpm record player and not following the schedule. But Phillip later told me that what Roshi had said to him was, "Don't fight with Dick Baker!"

Phillip said, "I don't fight with Dick Baker!"

Roshi said, "Did you hear me? I said, 'Don't fight with Dick Baker!'"

Then he started hitting him with one of his Zen sticks. After a while, the stick broke. So Roshi got another stick, but Phillip took it away from him. He said, "Suzuki Roshi, these sticks are really precious. You don't want to break another one on me. I'm not worth it."

(An amusing sequel to this story is that Roshi asked our master carpenter Paul Discoe to repair the stick, but "not too well." Then when the Japanese priests came to visit, he planned to impress them by breaking the stick on the shoulders of one of his students.)

Phillip later said that while Roshi was hitting him, his energy kept getting bigger and bigger. He said, "I don't know if that's what was supposed to happen, but my energy was getting larger and larger—bigger than the room—really huge."

Roshi saw people's hearts. He saw Phillip's heart. He saw my heart. Ultimately, we're all like misfits, like in Rujing's poem "The Great Road." Somehow "we meet like misfits or bandits of the dharma." Each of us, in our way, is something of a misfit and something of a bandit. None of us is a perfect being.

It is so important for us to have a practice like this and a community and friends and support, because it is really challenging to be a human being. Thank you for being here and practicing with each other.

Wherever I Go, I Meet Myself

Zen Master Tozan said, "I meet myself wherever I go. As I proceed through the world, I meet myself wherever I go." Still, it's not a self he already knew, but a self appearing on each occasion.

How will we meet ourselves? Sometimes I long for my birth mother, who died when I was three years old, and I meet myself through that longing—through how that event made the life that I live.

And with that, I have a poem for you. This is from a letter that my mother wrote to her sister on April 1, 1948. My mother died on April 8, 1948, a week later.

This poem is from that ultra-smart magazine *The New Yorker*. In the poem "The Little Duck" by Donald C. Babcock, the poet observes a duck riding the waves far out beyond the surf. "He can rest while the Atlantic heaves, because he rests in the Atlantic." And what does he do even though he has no idea how large the ocean is? "He sits down in it. He reposes in

the immediate as if it were infinity—which it
is. That is religion, and the little duck has it."[62]

The letter from my mother continues, "There you are, Hattie. In other words, let's rest today. Rest calmly without worry, without fear. Take no thought of the morrow. Let's rest today as if it were infinity. Because it is." She was getting ready to die.

As are we. Moment after moment, just each thing, swelling up.

62   Donald C. Babcock, "The Little Duck," *The New Yorker*, October 4, 1947, 39.

Small Acts with Great Kindness

There are some very simple and profound ways to help ourselves wake up. How we really come alive is by doing things, by handling things. It is an important aspect of Zen. We come alive by doing and meeting things, taking care of things. We come alive by responding to one another.

So, "Do not be careful about one thing and careless about another . . . Do not give away your opportunity even if it is merely a drop in the ocean of merit; do not fail to place even a single particle of earth at the summit of the mountain of wholesome deeds."[63] This is similar to Mother Teresa saying that we can only do small acts, but with great love, with great kindness.

Sometimes I am quite discouraged about the state of the world. Global warming appears real, you know. So what are we going to do? There are still small acts of kindness we can do each moment. We can avoid being careless and respond carefully to things. That may mean scrubbing the pots, cleaning the kitchen, washing the rice, or preparing the vegetables.

---

63   Eihei Dōgen, "Tenzo Kyōkun," *Moon in a Dewdrop*, 54.

It can also include serving the food or doing the dishes or taking care of one drop of water, one particle of Earth.

And I don't know if it is going to make all the difference, but I don't know what else to do. We have to do something, you see. Can we save the world? I don't know.

But we can take care of each drop of water and each particle of Earth. So, please take care of yourself and each other, being nourished by each thing, by each moment.

Each Moment
a New Life

"The important thing," Suzuki Roshi said,
"is simply to wake up. Wake up to your life."

Many people—not just Zen teachers—have mentioned that it's useful to be interested and curious about life. I want to share a passage from a lecture Suzuki Roshi gave called "Stand Up by the Ground."

> So there is nothing to rely on in our practice. But on the other hand, there is always something provided for you, always. According to the circumstances, you will have some aid to practice our way. Even the pain in your legs is an aid. By the pain you have, you practice our way . . . The pain is "it." "It" is everything, but at that time, "it" is some definite experience or particular trouble. "It" can be drowsiness; "it" can be hunger; "it" can be hot weather. So hot weather or nice cool weather, or hunger, or mosquitoes, or the pain in your legs can be an aid to your practice with which you can stand

226

up and establish your practice. So not only Buddha's teaching, but everything can be an aid to us.

Immo-ji means "things," and *immo-nin* is someone who is practicing zazen. "Someone practicing something"—that is reality. Or we could say, "Someone doing something." Then *immo* is a discontinuous, particular being which has form and color. But as Dōgen Zenji says, Zen practice is something continuous, something mixed up with everything.

If it is so, then "someone doing zazen" already includes everything. Someone cannot be separate from this world. Some action cannot exist without the background of the whole world, and some thing cannot be apart from other things. So "someone," "doing," and "something" is the same thing, you know.

If they are the same thing, then we can say "something," "something," "something." What is that? That is complete realization. Everything happens in this way. So if you stick to the idea of help or enlightenment, that is already a mistake. You have separated yourself from everything.

Someone may attain enlightenment when he sees a flower or hears a sound. Someone may attain enlightenment when taking a hot bath or going to the restroom. Rich and poor may attain enlightenment in various ways. So actually there is not a Sōtō way or a Rinzai way.

We have discussed practice rather abstractly, but this is what it means: whatever it is, we should accept it. By various means moment after moment, we practice our way. There is no other way to attain enlightenment.[64]

And then there is this poem by Juan Ramón Jiménez:

> I have a feeling that my boat
> has struck, down there in the depths,
> against a great thing.
> And nothing
> happens! Nothing . . . Silence . . . Waves . . .
>
> Nothing happens? Or has everything happened,
> and are we standing now, quietly, in the new life?[65]

This has to do with our awareness and our willingness to receive a new moment, a moment that has never happened before. To fully receive this fresh moment, we need to not be too quick to make it something we know all about. Each moment is a new life.

---

64 *Not Always So*, 141–142.
65 Juan Ramón Jiménez, "Oceans," *Lorca & Jiménez: Selected Poems*, trans. Robert Bly (Boston: Beacon Press, 1973), 63.

Afterword

To the extent
I am aware that I am in the middle of some things,
Chewing, stewing, moving along, I have resources

More than ever I am aware that I am flying freely
Connected to the core of the earth
And yet, receiving high heaven
One with the vastness, loved and loving . . .

Yet, time is short
Life passes in a flash

A few moments and a couple of days ago,
I was working in the Tassajara kitchen above the pit.
You know, that kitchen?

A few moments from now,
you will be doing my memorial service.

And a few moments later Suzuki Roshi
will walk in the door . . .

Acknowledgments

Edward Espe Brown has been teaching and speaking about Zen practice and spiritual liberation for more than forty years. Thus, the body of work to be reviewed was extensive.

Many individuals and institutions provided recordings that made up the mountain of available material. They include the San Francisco Zen Center and its affiliated centers, Green Gulch Farm Zen Center and Tassajara Zen Mountain Center. Thanks also to Spirit Rock Meditation Center for permission to use talks from this location, as well as others from the Sacramento Buddhist Meditation Group, Chapel Hill Zen Center, and Puregg Haus der Stille in Austria.

Within this process, I very much appreciate Charlie Wilson's very professional conversion of the many cassette tapes, CDs, and even reel-to-reel recordings to an MP3 format. These were instrumental to our progress. Indeed, Charlie's effort made our book possible.

This work has evolved through an effort by many individuals over the last four years. First and foremost, as editor, I appreciate the vital help from Sally Harris Sange, who transcribed over ninety of the approximately three hundred and fifty talks spanning twenty-five years, which we selected after an extensive review. These were then cooked down again.

Beyond the painstaking work associated with transcription, Sally also helped me with editing and selecting the final material, as well as sharing comments and suggestions for the draft manuscript. She knows how instrumental she was to the results. My deepest thanks and gratitude.

These talks were often heavily edited for length and substance and then organized into topics for the book. Those wishing to examine the original lectures are encouraged to do so. It should be noted that, as with many speakers, Ed Brown often evokes obvious emotion, humor, and deep feeling in the spoken word that is difficult to capture here. We plan to establish a web link to a number of the talks for those who have that interest (peacefulseasangha.com/audio/audio.htm).

I appreciate input and recollections from David Chadwick (cuke.com), filmmaker Doris Dörrie, and Mathias Köhl at the Buddhistches Zentrum Scheibbs. I further wish to thank others for helpful review or suggestions for the material: Valorie Beer, Colleen Morton Busch, Anne Hinckle, and Marjorie Walter. Clare Hollander provided very helpful notes taken on many of Ed's talks, which were otherwise unrecorded, and my friend Helene Zindarsian shared photographs. Margot Koch helped me to sort through stacks of pictures, diaries, and years of detailed notebooks. Thomas Radlwimmer (www.radlwimmer.at/) contributed the stunning photograph that graces the book's cover.

Many thanks also to my agent Katherine Fausset at Curtis Brown, who has unfailingly represented me with deft ability over the years. At Sounds True, appreciation for the patient assistance of Caroline Pincus to help produce a memorable and handsome work. We also appreciate the skill of editors Jade Lascelles and Vesela Simic in the production process.

I also thank my dear friend John Busch, who has helped me in ways difficult to tell: mysterious synchronicity. His friendship and encouragement have meant so much over the years.

Finally, my appreciation to Edward Espe Brown himself, to whom I owe special gratitude for his teachings and his trust. Thank you.

May the merit of our collective effort extend everywhere.

DSP

Sources of Teachings

"Wild West Tassajara" adapted from "What You Think Is Not a Help for Realization," recorded at Tassajara Zen Mountain Center on May 11, 2010.

"Easy Is Right" adapted from "Tasting the True Spirit of the Grain," recorded at Sacramento Buddhist Meditation Group on January 21, 2007.

"Tasting the True Spirit of the Grain" adapted from "Tasting the True Spirit of the Grain," recorded at Sacramento Buddhist Meditation Group on January 21, 2007.

"Rotten Pickles" adapted from "Tasting the True Spirit of the Grain," recorded at Sacramento Buddhist Meditation Group on January 21, 2007.

"You Might As Well Dance" adapted from "You Might As Well Dance," recorded at Green Gulch Farm Zen Center on March 24, 2002.

"True Calm Is Not What You Thought" adapted from "True Calm Is Not What You Thought," recorded at Spirit Rock Meditation Center on February 27, 2000.

"The Benefits of Meditation" adapted from "Finding Out What You Really Want," recorded at Tassajara Zen Mountain Center on July 29, 1988.

"A Misbehaving Egg" adapted from "Finding Out What You Really Want," recorded at Tassajara Zen Mountain Center on July 29, 1988.

"Rujing, the Great Road, and the Bandits of Dharma" adapted from "Rujing, the Great Road, and the Bandits of Dharma," recorded at Spirit Rock Meditation Center on April 24, 2006.

"Two Demons at the Door" adapted from "Two Demons Pushing on the Door," recorded at Green Gulch Farm Zen Center on July 11, 2009.

"Offer What You Have to Offer" adapted from "Telling Our Deepest Darkest Secrets," recorded at Green Gulch Farm Zen Center on February 10, 2008.

"The Light in the Darkness" adapted from "Offering What You Can Offer," recorded at Spirit Rock Meditation Center on December 30, 2002.

"Even a Thousands Sages Can't Say" adapted from "Even a Thousand Sages Can't Say," recorded at Green Gulch Farm Zen Center on June 14, 1998.

"The Gift of Attention" adapted from "The Gift of Attention," recorded at Green Gulch Farm Zen Center on April 18, 2009.

"Finding What You Really Want" adapted from "Finding Out What You Really Want," recorded at Tassajara Mountain Zen Center on July 29, 1988.

"Accepting Yourself Completely" adapted from "Accepting Yourself Completely," recorded at Green Gulch Farm Zen Center on September 4, 1999.

"Just Go Ahead" adapted from "Just Go Ahead," recorded at Tassajara Zen Mountain Center on August 4, 1999.

"The Backward Step" adapted from "The Backward Step," recorded at Tassajara Zen Mountain Center on July 30, 2000.

"Everything Is Coming from Beyond" adapted from "Everything Is Coming from Beyond," recorded at Valley Streams Zen Sangha on October 28, 2013.

"Physical Challenges" adapted from "Everything Is Coming from Beyond," recorded at Valley Streams Zen Sangha on October 28, 2013.

"Informed by a Daffodil" adapted from "Informed by a Daffodil," recorded at Tassajara Zen Mountain Center on August 13, 2003.

"Virtue and a Cook's Temperament" adapted from "Virtue and a Cook's Temperament," recorded at Cambridge Insight Meditation Center on May 14, 1993.

"In Search of the Perfect Biscuit" adapted from "Making the Perfect Biscuit," recorded at Green Gulch Farm Zen Center on October 17, 2012.

"Coffee Meditation" reprinted from "A Jolt of Meditation" by Edward Espe Brown, *Yoga Journal*, Sept.–Oct. 2001.

"Honoring Leftovers" adapted from "Don't Waste Even One Grain of Rice," recorded at Tassajara Zen Mountain Center on July 16, 2006.

"Dreaming of Pizza: A Talk for Children" adapted from "Thinking of Pizza," recorded at Green Gulch Farm Zen Center on February 2, 2003.

"Thanksgiving and Gratitude" adapted from "Thanksgiving and Gratitude," recorded at Green Gulch Farm Zen Center on November 21, 1993.

"Don't Put Another Head Above Your Own" adapted from "Enjoy Your Food," recorded at Green Gulch Farm Zen Center on June 8, 1997.

"The Ten Thousand Idiots" adapted from "The Ten Thousand Idiots," recorded at Spirit Rock Meditation Center on March 26, 2007.

"Subtle Feeling Reveals Illumination" adapted from "The Ten Thousand Idiots," recorded at Spirit Rock Meditation Center on March 26, 2007.

"Sitting with Tragedy" adapted from "Sitting with Tragedy," recorded at Green Gulch Farm Zen Center on December 16, 2012.

"Rohatsu" adapted from "Sitting with Tragedy," recorded at Green Gulch Farm Zen Center on December 16, 2012.

"Zen Practice and Meeting Early Childhood Trauma" adapted from "The Importance of Problems in Your Practice," recorded at Green Gulch Farm Zen Center on July 18, 2010.

"Confronting War and Uncertainty" adapted from "Confronting War and Uncertainty," recorded at Green Gulch Farm Zen Center on February 2, 2003.

"The Secret to Life" adapted from "The Secret to Life— Enjoyment," recorded at Spirit Rock Meditation Center on August 6, 2001.

"Enjoyment, Excitement, Greed, and Lust" adapted from "The Secret to Life—Enjoyment," recorded at Spirit Rock Meditation Center on August 6, 2001.

"When Is Adversity Useful?" adapted from "When Is Adversity Useful?" recorded at Green Gulch Farm Zen Center on November 3, 2013.

"Bugs in a Bowl" adapted from "Bugs in a Bowl," recorded at Tassajara Zen Mountain Center on July 26, 2004.

"Is My Practice Working?" is an undated talk found among Ed Brown's personal papers.

"Beginner's Mind" adapted from "The Importance of Problems in Practice," recorded at Green Gulch Farm Zen Center on July 18, 2010.

"What Was Said to the Rose" adapted from "The Thread," recorded at Green Gulch Farm Zen Center on October 7, 2007.

"Bewildered?" came from notes from an unrecorded talk at Green Gulch Farm Zen Center, no date.

"No Masterpieces, Just Cooking" adapted from "No Masterpieces, Just Cooking," recorded at Green Gulch Farm Zen Center on January 26, 1992.

"Soft Mind" adapted from "Soft Mind," recorded at Green Gulch Farm Zen Center in the summer of 1997.

"Misfits" adapted from "Everyone Making Their Best Effort," recorded at Tassajara Zen Mountain Center on May 13, 2009.

"Wherever I Go, I Meet Myself" adapted from "Good Enough for Me," recorded at Green Gulch Farm Zen Center on September 25, 1988.

"Small Acts with Great Kindness" adapted from "Small Acts with Great Kindness," recorded at Tassajara Zen Mountain Center on May 16, 2005.

"Each Moment a New Life" adapted from "How To Be You," recorded at Green Gulch Farm Zen Center on August 9, 2008.

Permissions

About the Author and the Editor

Edward Espe Brown is a Sōtō Zen priest in the lineage of the legendary teacher Shunryu Suzuki (*Zen Mind, Beginner's Mind*). In 1971, Suzuki ordained Edward, giving him the name *Jusan Kainei*, meaning "Longevity Mountain, Peaceful Sea."

Widely known in the United States and Europe for his meditation and cooking classes, Edward is the author of several books, among them *The Tassajara Bread Book*, published in 1970, an international phenomenon that inspired a generation to bake and cook. He has taught Zen practice for more than forty years, utilizing yoga sessions and more recently qi gong classes for students to have a fuller flow of energy and vitality.

In 2007, Doris Dörrie made a feature-length film about Edward called *How to Cook Your Life*. Sounds True published his most recent book, *No Recipe*, in May 2018.

Danny Parker is a longtime student of Edward's and was ordained by him in 2011 and given the Buddhist name *Shōjō Reigen* (Deep Listening, Sacred Ground). Danny's day job is to study residential energy efficiency—how to reach zero energy houses. Along with this work and raising a family, he has completed several books about the Second World War, including most recently *Hitler's Warrior*—a character study of how racial intolerance and war can be tragically embraced by society. Edward attests that Danny is an unusual sweetheart of a person and a joy for people to be around.

About Sounds True

Sounds True is a multimedia publisher whose mission is to inspire and support personal transformation and spiritual awakening. Founded in 1985 and located in Boulder, Colorado, we work with many of the leading spiritual teachers, thinkers, healers, and visionary artists of our time. We strive with every title to preserve the essential "living wisdom" of the author or artist. It is our goal to create products that not only provide information to a reader or listener, but that also embody the quality of a wisdom transmission.

For those seeking genuine transformation, Sounds True is your trusted partner. At SoundsTrue.com you will find a wealth of free resources to support your journey, including exclusive weekly audio interviews, free downloads, interactive learning tools, and other special savings on all our titles.

To learn more, please visit SoundsTrue.com/freegifts or call us toll-free at 800.333.9185.